Babyworks

Every Parent's Sourcebook
For Essential Baby Paraphernalia

Jean Mills

VIKING

VIKING
Viking Penguin Inc.,
40 West 23rd Street,
New York, New York 10010, U.S.A.

First published in 1985

A QUARTO BOOK

ISBN 0-670-80838-5

Library of Congress Catalog Card Number: 85-40537
(C.I.P. data available)

BABYWORKS: *Every Parent's Sourcebook for Essential
Baby Paraphernalia*
was prepared and produced by
Quarto Marketing Ltd.
15 West 26th Street
New York, New York 10010

Editor: Karla Olson
Designer: Mary Moriarty
Photo Researcher: Susan M. Duane

Typeset by BPE Graphics, Inc.
Color separations by Hong Kong Scanner Craft Company Ltd.
Printed and bound in Hong Kong by Leefung-Asco Printers Ltd.

Set in Futura Light

The publisher is not responsible for the safety standards of any of
the products recommended in this book, though in some cases the
manufacturers are required to meet federal regulations. However,
please be sure to obtain and review all manufacturer's
specifications and safety information, notices, or instructions
before you make a purchase or use any of these products.

DEDICATION

To my mother and father

ACKNOWLEDGMENTS

I'd especially like to thank David and Naomi Black; Mindy Isacoff at Lewis of London; Susan Astor at The Playorena; Joanna O'Connell at Mothercare Stores; Albee Baby Carriage Co., Inc.; Judy, Scott, and their baby, Kate, for their expert advice; Kathy Faust for helping me get organized; Todd and Robert Mills, Janet Brady, Margaret Murphy, Mike Gustafson, and Bender's fifth floor for their encouragement.

CONTENTS

INTRODUCTION

Contact. The first tender touch of the baby's cheek on yours thrillingly projects you into a brand new world of sensory awareness—the incomparable world of parenthood. Incredibly demanding, yet fantastically rewarding, it is nonetheless a world filled to overflowing with a number of mind boggling choices.

To deal intelligently with these choices, which range from objects designed to induce play all the way to objets d'art designed to induce investment, parents are sure to need, at the very least, daring and imagination, and at the very most, all of the information they can gather. Each choice you make will undeniably affect your child, not only today, but more subtly in the future as well.

The months of your pregnancy were profoundly important ones, but the world you're entering now, the world of a baby's first touches, sights, and sounds, are equally important and infinitely more challenging. Never before has the array of infant paraphernalia been so wide, so varied, or so expensive, whether it is a simple cradle bath you're purchasing or a Galway crystal bottle. Yet, as dear as some of the items may seem, none are so priceless as the baby entrusted to your loving care.

Because this childhood world is so special, and because of the awareness which it engenders, this book has been created to help you, the parent, deal, not by trial and error but sensibly and sensitively, with the decisions you face at this very moment.

In a painstaking search for excellence, with you and your baby's best interest in mind, an impressive list of infant accouterments has been assembled. In choosing items, the fundamental qualities of service and dependability have been combined with the traditional values of long-lasting beauty and treasurability—in a phrase, practicality with a designer look. Time savers, high performance, easy-care instructions, aesthetics, and the often overwhelming desire to indulge your child were all factors taken into account in the selection process.

In compiling the information for this book, manufacturers and retail store managers helped by providing the latest available product information, as well as the inside story on who buys what and why. Actual mothers and fathers were asked for their product recommendations and for their advice on safety, health care, timesaving ideas, and more. These helpful hints from sources in the know are highlighted throughout the chapters. The checklists in each chapter provide information in a concise form that's easy to consult before you make a purchase.

The following pages are replete with choices, but choices with a difference—choices made in order to free a busy parent's time so that sustaining and loving your child is less trying and more pleasurable. It's an ambitious but worthy project, guaranteed to add a little common sense and a lot of magic to your world of parenthood.

1

FIRST THINGS FIRST

LAYETTE ESSENTIALS

A few months before a newborn's arrival, mothers often experience sudden and exciting bursts of energy. Tangible, material preparations for the baby become top priorities as the mother eagerly begins to acknowledge the actuality of the approaching birth.

Assembling a layette for your baby-to-be is often part of the result of this "nesting" instinct. A layette includes all of the basic clothing, linen, feeding, and bathing needs that will help get your baby through the first few months of life. You'll find yourself shopping for baby's new clothes, or maybe even trying to make your own, but for almost every pregnant woman, preparing a layette is a satisfying and enjoyable experience.

Before you get carried away, however, there are a few things that you should look for and remember. The first is that, hopefully, you'll never need to buy everything on a layette list, because you'll probably receive many items as gifts. In purchasing clothing, you should look for features that accommodate growth. Adjustable snaps or buttons, tucks, and seams that can be let out often make good sense. Linens should be soft so they are pleasing to your baby, in fabrics that are absorbent and washable for your convenience.

LAYETTE ESSENTIALS

CLOTHES	SUGGESTED QUANTITY
• stretchies	4-8
• kimonos	3
• drawstring gowns	3-6
• t-shirts	6-10
• diaper sets	4
• sweaters	1-3
• blanket sleepers	3
• bunting or pram suit	1
• booties	3
• hats	1-2
• cloth diapers or disposable diapers	2-4 dozen

LINEN	
• receiving blankets	3-6
• crib sheets	4-6
• waterproof sheets	6
• crib blanket	2-3
• crib bumpers	1 set
• towels	3-5
• washcloths	4-6
• bibs	4-6

OTHER NEEDS	
• bottles	2 or more if breastfeeding; 8 if bottlefeeding
• pacifiers	
• diaper bag	
• portable bath	
• brush/comb set	
• baby scissors	

PARENTS ADVISE

Remember not to use any bar soap, liquid soap, or soap powder when washing flame-resistant clothing. There's a soap buildup that stays after washing and can ruin the fabric. It smells bad and makes the sleeper stiff.—JBM

CLOTHING

STRETCHIES OR JUMPSUITS

One of the largest parts of a baby's wardrobe consists of stretchies or jumpsuits suitable for wearing year-round and for both sleeping and playtime. They usually come with feet, so be careful not to buy them too small. Also, look for suits with snaps or zippers that extend down one leg, so diapers can be easily changed. Stretchies are considered sleepwear, so federal regulations require that they be made of flame-resistant fabric.

The simple, classic lines of **Marimekko Sleepsuits** give your little one a chic and adorable style. They're soft and comfortable in a "Snowflower" or "Bo-Boo" (cars and trucks) design. They are made of 100 percent Fortrel polyester.

A sleeveless, snap-shoulder, snap-up the leg **Stretchie** from **Lion's Baby** comes in cheerful prints of balloons, hearts, or stars on a white background. This sexy little number can be dressed up with a long-sleeved t-shirt underneath. Or, for warm summer days, your baby can wear it alone. It is 100 percent cotton.

For the fastest change in the west, north, east, and south, try the **Pilucho Stretchie** from **J. C. Penney.** It's a diaper-style wraparound that unsnaps fully for easy diaper access. There are double rows of snaps allowing for growth, and the fabric's softness wraps your baby with tender care. The Pilucho is available in either long or short sleeves and can be worn alone or as an undergarment. It comes in 100 percent soft cotton rib knit or terry.

KIMONOS

Kimonos are open-front nighties that snap at the neck and are either waist-length or full-length. They have short sleeves and do not close at the bottom—like drawstring gowns do—which makes them appropriate for spring or summer wear.

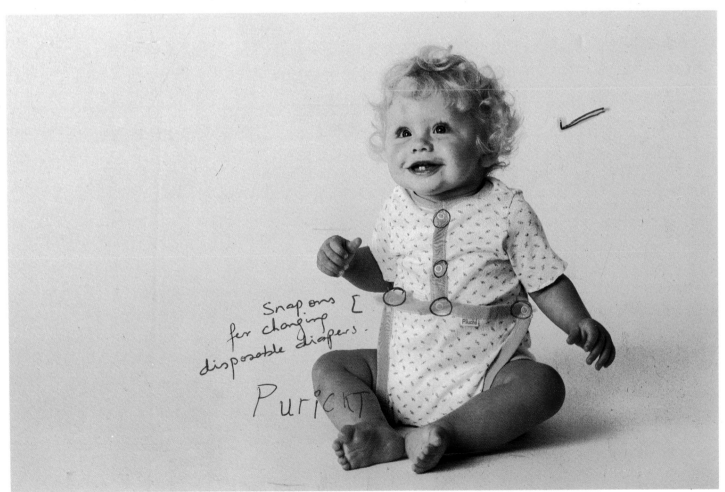

PILUCHO STRETCHIE BY J.C. PENNEY

Because kimonos are used as sleepwear, they should be made of flame-resistant material.

In a confetti-dot-and-rocking-horse design, a full-length **Kimono** from **Gerber Products** makes diaper changes a breeze. The front snaps shut; one size fits newborns up to thirteen pounds.

Carter's features a playful, comfy, open-front **Kimono.** The two snaps on the front are adorned with tiny, delicate white bows. The Kimono is available in pastel colors, white, and selected prints.

DRAWSTRING GOWNS

Like stretchies, baby gowns are year-round garments. They snap at the neck and have draft-free drawstring bottoms that can be opened or closed depending on the season. Mitten sleeves can also be left opened or closed to prevent your baby from scratching his or her face. When purchasing baby gowns, be sure to check that they are made of flame-resistant material.

You'll love to cuddle your baby in **Absorba's** cozy little **Drawstring Gowns.** Snaps at the neck make it easy to pull

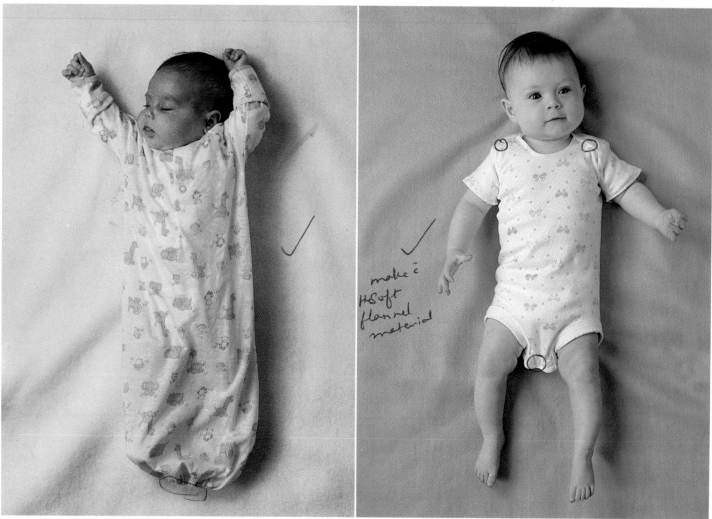

DRAWSTRING GOWN AND DIAPER SET BY CARTER'S

the gown over the baby's head and the drawstring is removable to accommodate a baby's growth. They are available in a variety of Absorba's adorable designs in cotton/polyester flame-resistant fabric.

Mothercare Stores has responded to a baby's blossoming needs by offering a roomy **"Bunny Capers" Baby Gown** in one size that fits babies up to sixteen pounds. Mitten sleeves gently tuck in baby's hands and a matching "Bunny Capers" bonnet is also available, all in durable, machine-washable 100 percent polyester.

In addition to baby gowns, **Mothercare Stores** offers a **Complete Layette Collection** that includes bonnets and booties, stretchies, t-shirts, pram suits, and much, much more. Made either from all cotton or flame-resistant polyester for sleepwear, the layette items are practical and affordable. They are also extremely fashionable, as they are updated seasonally with the latest European styles. In addition to pastel bunny designs, a whimsical bear-and-dot pattern in bright colors is available. To avoid duplications in gift buying, or to keep your baby's wardrobe straight, Mothercare offers a layette registry at any of their over 400 stores.

COMPLETE LAYETTE COLLECTION BY MOTHERCARE STORES

T-SHIRTS

Until your baby is several months old, it's a good idea to use side-snap t-shirts. Later on, you may want to switch to a wide-neck pullover style; however, V-necks and side snaps facilitate a baby's many dress changes in the course of the day. Both styles are almost always made of 00 percent cotton, so they are comfortable, lightweight, and absorbent.

When selecting t-shirts, look for seamless underarms to prevent unpleasant chafing on your baby's tender skin.

Lion's Baby offers a long-sleeved, side-snap **T-Shirt** in adorable little balloons, hearts, or stars prints that coordinate with the company's stretchies. A matching diaper cover is also available. The t-shirt is V-neck with long sleeves, so it is a

Top snaps prevent pulling dress over the head. So go for this or any other alternative — please you

DIAPER SET AND STRETCHIE BY LION'S BABY

versatile piece suitable for both warm and cool weather. It is made of 100 percent cotton.

Up, up, and away! **Visions** of New York City makes original airbrushed design **T-Shirts** with colorful balloons drifting among the clouds. T-shirts are available with long or short sleeves, as tank-tops or adorable little T-shirt dresses. A number of other custom designs are available, including "City Skyline," "Sailboats," and "Palmtree Sunrise," or send in a rough draft of your own personal design. Sleepers, diaper sets, ankle socks, and other layette wear are available. All designs are done on 100 percent cotton, except the sleepwear, which is on a cotton/polyester blend. The paints are non-toxic, and the entire collection is machine washable.

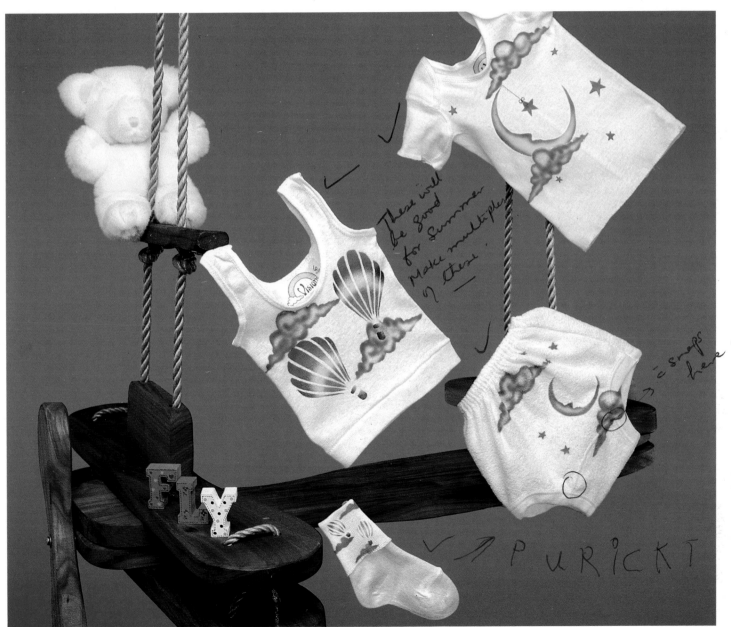

DIAPER SET BY VISIONS

If you're planning to use cloth diapers, you may want to consider **Carter's T-Shirts** with attached diaper tabs. Pin the diaper to the tabs and pull the t-shirt down to cover them. Carters' tabs are made of antiwicking material, so they won't twist. The tabs will prevent the t-shirt from riding up on your baby, thus keeping out unwanted drafts.

DIAPER SETS

Diaper sets are usually worn during the summer months and are often considered playtime outfits. Basically, the set includes a pullover, lap-shouldered t-shirt with matching panties wide enough to cover the diaper. There are, however, variations upon this theme. A sacque set, for example, has a snap front with short raglan sleeves and a matching diaper cover which also snaps for easy changes. A "creeper" is a pullover one-piece suit with a snap-fastened neck and crotch.

Absorba's Diaper Sets feature wide-neck, lap-shoulder pullover t-shirts that make it easy for you—and comfortable for your baby—to put on. The matching panties are cool, lightweight, and snug, so droopy diapers won't stick out. They're 100 percent cotton in an assortment of Absorba's charming patterns.

A polka-dot, side-snap t-shirt and matching bottoms make up **Spencer's Diaper Set**. There's no pulling or tugging to get it on; simply lay the shirt flat, lay baby onto it, bring his or her arms through, and snap the shirt on front. Panties slip on easily, too, with a wide-bottom diaper cover. The sets are made from a cotton/polyester blend in a variety of prints.

SWEATERS AND HATS

For the cold weather months or for cool weather in the early spring or fall, it's a good idea to have a few sweaters and hats on hand. Button-down and machine-washable sweaters are the most practical, but you may want to include a handmade woolen one in your baby's wardrobe.

Ducks, boats, hearts, and flowers are just a few of the designs available in these adorable **Sweater and Hat Sets** from **The Maine Madhatter**. The company offers warm, toasty mittens and matching hats with ear covers. Of 100 percent acrylic, the washable sets are made to last. They are available in small (6 months) to medium (12 months) sizes at Bellini's.

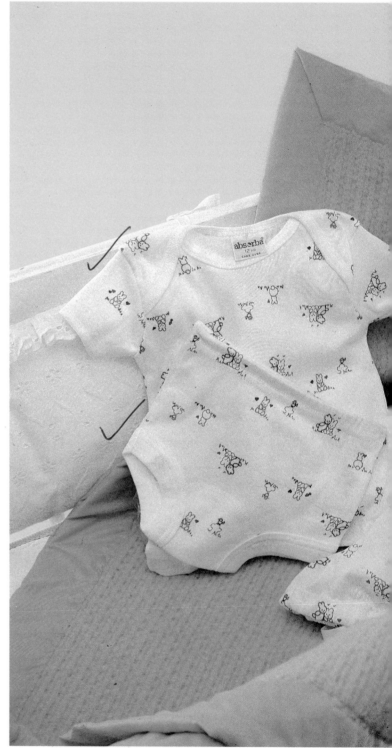

DIAPER SET AND DRAWSTRING GOWN BY ABSORBA

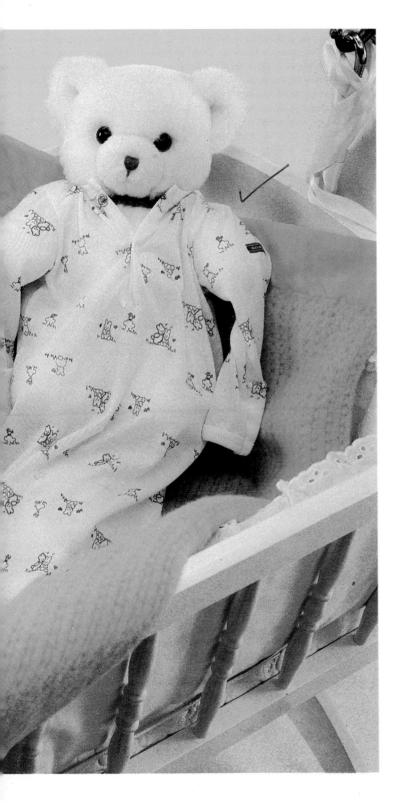

Useful for summer, early fall.

DIAPER SETS BY SPENCER

PARENTS ADVISE

Hats that tie under the chin are usually the most uncomfortable style for babies.—PJB

BLANKET SLEEPERS

Blanket sleepers are available with legs and without legs. The style without legs is called a sleeping bag and often has grow seams—seams that can be taken out as the baby gets bigger—at the bottom. The sleepers come in lightweight and heavyweight fabric and are ideal if the baby kicks off the covers on a chilly night. Although some blanket sleepers are heavy enough to be used as bunting or pram suits, a stretchie or baby gown can be worn underneath for greater warmth.

Assure your baby a cuddly, warm, restful night's sleep with **Carter's** medium-or heavyweight brushed **Sleeping Bags.** Seamless underarms, mitten sleeves and grow seams at the bottom are practical, functional features that make Carter's sleeping bags a fine choice. A snap-neck tab and two-way zipper make changing easier, too. They're available in white, colors, or prints and are made of 100 percent polyester that meets federal safety standards.

BUNTINGS OR PRAM SUITS

For travel or carriage in cold weather, you'll need a bunting or a pram suit (also called a snowsuit) for the baby. A bunting resembles a sleeping bag in that it doesn't have legs, while pram suits do. They're both made of heavy fabric and most of them have hoods and mittens. Zippers on pram suits usually extend down the leg, while zippers on buntings are at the sides or down the front of the bag. Either way makes inserting your baby easy.

A **Convertible Suit** from **Tidykins** is both snowsuit and bunting in one. It's quilted for greater warmth and comfort, and features mittened sleeves and a fleecy pile-lined hood. They're available, at Saks Fifth Avenue and other department stores, in a variety of colors with different embroidered Peter Rabbit designs on the front.

◆◆◆◆◆◆◆◆◆◆◆◆◆◆◆◆◆◆◆◆◆◆◆◆◆◆◆◆

PARENTS ADVISE

If mittens button to the sleeves on pram suits, sew them on so you won't lose them.—MMM

◆◆◆◆◆◆◆◆◆◆◆◆◆◆◆◆◆◆◆◆◆◆◆◆◆◆◆◆

For preppy babies, try the **Izod Lacoste Snowsuit** in eyecatching pink corduroy. The interior quilted lining is adorned with pink diamonds and circles on a white background. It's a cheerful, sporty style with a hood and mittens that button onto the sleeves. The suit is made from a heavyweight cotton/polyester blend and has a zipper that extends from neck to crotch.

BOOTIES

Booties keep your baby's feet warm in cool weather, but your highest priority in buying them should be the proper fit. The bones in babies' feet are still undeveloped—in fact they aren't completely developed until the twentieth year of life. Confining booties—even tight stockings—may inhibit the proper growth of your infant's feet and should, therefore, be avoided.

Booties by **Mothercare Stores** come in adorable pastel bunny prints. Ribbon ties keep the booties from falling off, but do not bind the baby's feet. The booties are pretty and functional, and are made of a cotton/polyester blend.

DIAPERS

Parents have basically two choices when it comes to diapers: cloth or disposable. **Cloth Diapers** are cheaper, but leave much to be desired when it comes to form-fitting style. Some advantages, however, are that you can hire a diaper service for a relatively small fee to take care of laundering hassles, and with cloth diapers, the frequency of diaper rash is lower. Even if you do choose disposable diapers, you should have half a dozen cloth diapers on hand for burping pads, area pads, or just for cleaning up.

◆◆◆◆◆◆◆◆◆◆◆◆◆◆◆◆◆◆◆◆◆◆◆◆◆◆◆◆

PARENTS ADVISE

Changing time should be a special time to talk or play with your baby. Make it enjoyable. Sing, give baby a book to "read" or a small toy to play with.—KLF

◆◆◆◆◆◆◆◆◆◆◆◆◆◆◆◆◆◆◆◆◆◆◆◆◆◆◆◆

Disposable Diapers are more expensive, but they're the most convenient, especially if you're working outside the home. Disposables revolutionized diaper changing by offering an attractive alternative to the traditional waterproof pants over cloth diapers. Disposables consist of thick absorbent padding between two outer water-resistant plastic linings. The newest designs feature even thicker, more absorbent padding, elastic legs for a snug fit, and tapes that can be refastened. **Huggies, Luvs,** and **Pampers** are all examples of this versatile type of disposable diaper.

DIAPER BAGS

For carrying anything and everything—diapers, bottles, food, extra clothing, or toys—you'll need a washable, durable, and roomy diaper bag. Drape it over your shoulder, loop it onto the stroller handles, but don't leave home without it.

Mothercare Stores Spring/Summer Diaper Bag has been designed with today's mothers in mind. Carefully styled according to the latest fashions in both maternity wear and the luggage industry, this diaper bag always looks great. But it's practical, too, featuring several roomy pockets and compartments for baby supplies and a ready-made changing pad that folds out. The Mothercare label is woven in for that final touch of class.

The **Snugli Diaper Bag** is a shoulder bag, handbag, backpack, and stroller bag all in one. It comes in colors to match the Snugli Soft Baby Carrier (see p.92). This amazing, versatile bag features a fold-out, washable changing pad and spacious inside and outside pockets. The entire bag is machine washable.

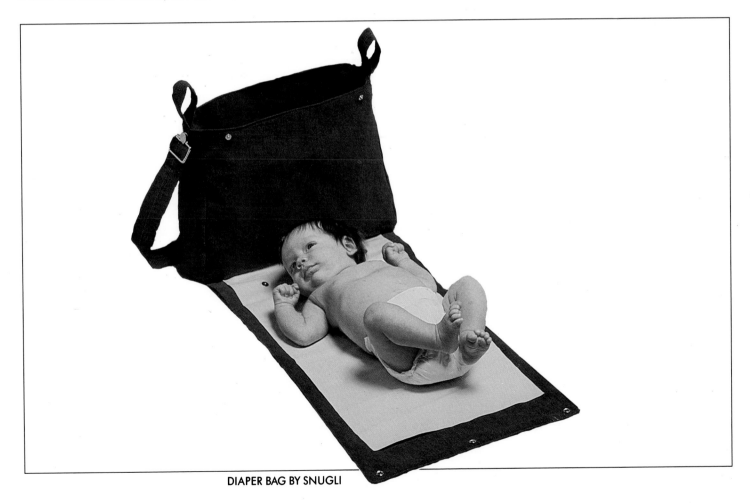

DIAPER BAG BY SNUGLI

L I N E N S

RECEIVING BLANKETS

These soft, lightweight, cotton blankets are often used to swaddle a newborn on the trip home from the hospital, and for holding or carrying the child during the next few weeks. They can also be used to cover an infant seat, as a lightweight blanket in a crib or stroller, or as a changing pad.

Lion's Baby offers a 100 percent cotton **Receiving Blanket** that will welcome your new heartthrob with softness and security. This protective wrap provides a soothing, caring feeling that babies need, especially during those first few weeks of life. It comes in one size, and is available in prints and solids.

CRIB SHEETS

Crib sheets should be fitted so you won't have to worry that they will become untucked. Sheets made of cotton or a

CRIB SETS BY MARIMEKKO

cotton-polyester blend are preferable for a newborn's tender skin; older babies will like ones with patterns or prints because they're fun to look at.

For the nursery, there's nothing smarter than **Marimekko's** ''Bo-Boo'' and ''Snowflower'' design **Crib Sets.** The bright primary colors in the famous snowflower and cars-and-trucks patterns will stimulate and please your baby, as well as provide soft, comfortable bedding. Sheets are fitted, machine washable, and require no ironing. In addition to the sheet, the entire set consists of a matching padded crib bumper, a comforter, and a pillow.

PARENTS ADVISE
Babies don't use pillows and you shouldn't place one in a crib. It's bad for posture and may cause suffocation.—LLS

WATERPROOF SHEETS

These are placed between the crib sheet and mattress to protect the mattress from baby's leaky diapers. They're rubberized, but have a soft, absorbent surface. You may want to place additional padding—a cloth diaper or quilted pad, or maybe a folded receiving blanket—beneath baby's head and bottom for extra protection against wetness. Waterproof pads are available in most department stores.

CRIB BLANKETS

In addition to receiving blankets, you'll need a few crib blankets or comforters for the baby's bedding. Lighter blankets are better for the summer and heavier ones for the winter, but washable blankets, no matter what the season, make the most sense. Make sure the baby doesn't get lost in a blanket that's too large. Knit blankets are often preferred because they conform to the baby's shape, making him feel cozy and secure.

Thermal Crib Blankets from **Carter's** provide lightweight warmth for a baby, making them suitable for both summer and winter nights. They'll keep an infant warm and snug and they're easy to care for. They are available with pastel or printed borders.

CRIB BUMPERS

Crib bumpers or guards line the inside of a crib and protect the baby from rolling against the hard surface of a crib. They're padded and usually come in printed soft cotton or cotton-blend fabric.

Marimekko includes **Crib Bumpers** in its ''Snowflower'' or ''Bo-Boo'' crib set, but if you're feeling crafty, you can easily make your own. **Laura Ashley** provides easy instructions for a **Crib or Cot Lining** in her *Book of Home Decorating* that makes a charming and cozy dressing for baby's crib.

2

SOFT TOUCH

LINENS FOR BABY

When purchasing linens, look for items that are practical enough to stand up to wear and tear and frequent washing, but are gentle and delicate enough for your baby's tender skin. Soft, cozy, durable linens will give your newborn a loving sense of protection and comfort. Natural fibers are the best—brushed cottons, soft flannels, or lambskins are ideal for a baby's peaceful night's sleep.

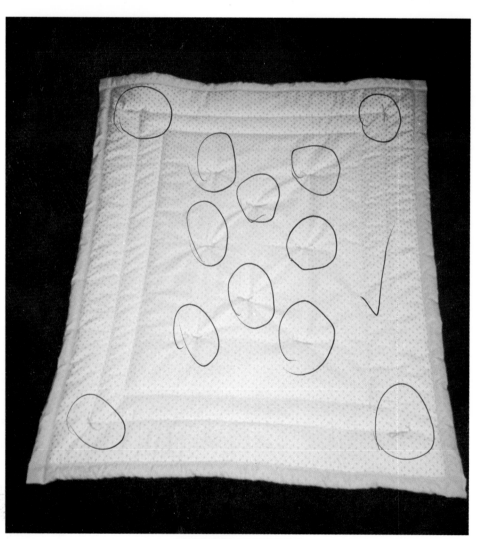

COMFORTER BY WEE CARE

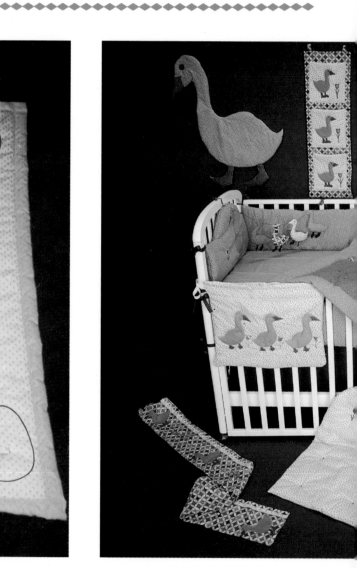

Create an abiding sense of tender loving care and comfort around your newborn. The quality and softness of 100 percent cotton flannel in handmade products from **Wee Care** is an undeniably great choice in **Linens** for your baby. The comforters are stuffed with batting and encased on all four sides with blanket binding or Wee Care's "Special Days" cotton crochet lace, which is quilted and pointed with satin ribbon. Bumper pads are also generously stuffed and suitable for both cradles and cribs. Fitted sheets and top sheets for cradles, cribs or portable cribs will keep your little one warm and toasty in the chilly months. An embroidered top binding

tastefully accents the total look of your infant's bedding. Nursing pads are eight layers thick, absorbent, and soft against your baby's skin. For the charm and quality that comes with handmade products, Wee Care's soft-touch approach to a baby's bedding is the answer.

Rainbow Artisans features twelve different irresistable designs to coordinate into a total look for your baby's nursery. **Crib Bumpers, Sheets, Pillow Shams, Coverlets, Wallhangings, Mobiles,** and more lend an interesting, lively look to any scheme you choose. The designs are machine-appliqued

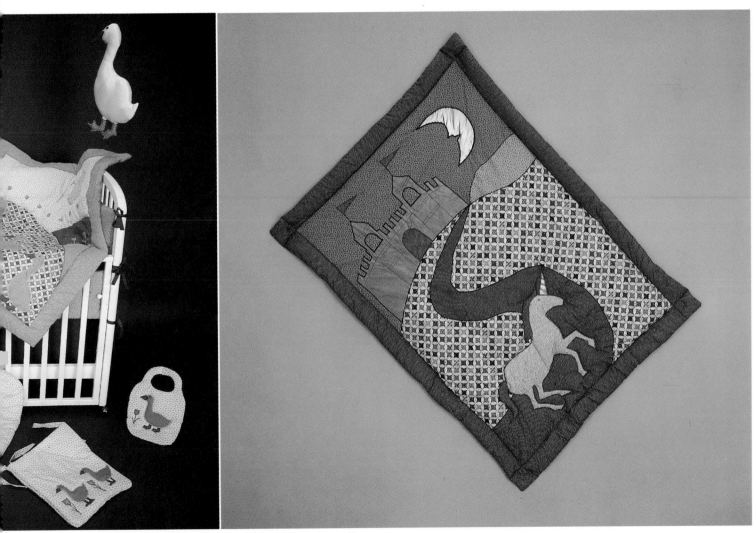

LINEN SET AND COVERLETS BY RAINBOW ARTISANS

onto charming ginghams, calicos, or pin dots, among many other fun fabrics. Made of 100 percent cotton, Rainbow Artisans' infant bedding and accessories are easy to care for.

Mothercare Stores is the world's largest retail chain store catering exclusively to the new parents. With over 400 stores throughout the United States, the United Kingdom, and the rest of Europe, Mothercare has certainly responded to the ever-increasing demands of busy mothers today. Durable, absorbent, gentle, Mothercare's **Linens** and **Nursery Coordinates** feature a fashionable designer look that's adaptable to your nursery decor. Easy-care comforters, baby blankets, crib and carriage sheets, bath sets, bibs, and bumper guards are all made from the finest materials. Choose a soft pastel,

bunny print or a cheerful, brightly colored bear pattern from Mothercare's own designer team.

Nursery Linens and **Coordinates** from **Pierre Deux** deserve special attention. Made from 100 percent cotton imported from France in hand-printed Provençal designs, Pierre Deux fabrics are synonymous with fine quality, elegance, and sophistication. These things can become a part of your baby's world from the start. Window dressings, canopies, dust ruffles, crib and cradle linens—everything can be adapted or custom-designed for your baby's nursery.

Rainbow Nursery Coordinates from **Red Calliope** will liven up your baby's room with a burst of bright colors, softness, and warmth. Yellow gingham fitted crib sheets are

NURSERY COORDINATES BY MOTHERCARE STORES

RAINBOW NURSERY COORDINATES BY RED CALLIOPE

 SOFT TOUCH

great at any age, but are especially adorable when they're accompanied by matching rainbow crib bumpers. Your child will delight in and be stimulated by the fluffy white clouds and bright colors of the rainbow wallhanging. Made from a cotton/polyester blend, sheets, bumpers, and wallhangings are conveniently machine washable.

Create a setting for your baby that's inviting, pleasant and compatible with **Nursery Coordinates** by **Noel Joanna.** A complete array of sheet sets, towel sets, crib bumpers and comforters, seat covers, wallhangings, dust ruffles, canopies, and much, much more is offered. Choose from a variety of cheerful and lovable designs. Stimulate your child's imagination with a "Storybook" design, or surround him or her in traditional charm with "Wedgwood Blue." "Royal T. Bear," "Animal Crackers," or "Bubbles The Whale" will become fast friends for your baby, or for a more understated beauty, try "Champagne Lace" or "Pastel Parfait" coordinates.

Handmade **Linens** and **Accessories** by **Glenna Jean** offer a variety of adorable designs to enhance any nursery decor. Quilts, bedding for cribs and cradles, bath sets, and more will surround your newborn with softness and comfort. Designs include colorful crayons, hippos, the softly shaded "Flower Garden," and "Jack in the Box," among others.

Baby's Best skillfully hand-crafted **Wallhangings** and **Pillows** by **Kamar** will add a charming, one-of-a-kind touch to your baby's nursery. Wake your baby up to the colorful sunrise wallhanging, or let dreams soar with the gentle pastel colors of the "Skyhigh Balloon." The "Gingerbread House Storybook" pillow is adorably delicious and a charming decoration for a crib.

Snuggles for baby! Your baby will have hours of nestling pleasure in **Domino Patchworks' Cuddly Comforters.** Colorful rainbows, sailboats, balloons, and more feed your baby's active imagination as well as stimulate sight and touch. Dacron-filled with a cotton/polyester blend exterior, the comforters are conveniently machine washable. Domino also makes crib bumpers, sheets, and bibs with a variety of designs for your selection.

Outfitting your newborn's nursery can be a darn good time with fun fabrics from **Gear Kids.** "Dancing Ducks," "Happy Critters," and a number of other patterns romp across the **Comforters, Sheets, Crib Bumpers, Pillowcases,** and more, filling your baby's new world with a cast of colorful characters. All items are comfy and fun to snuggle, and they're sturdily constructed and easy to care for.

LINENS AND ACCESSORIES BY GLENNA JEAN

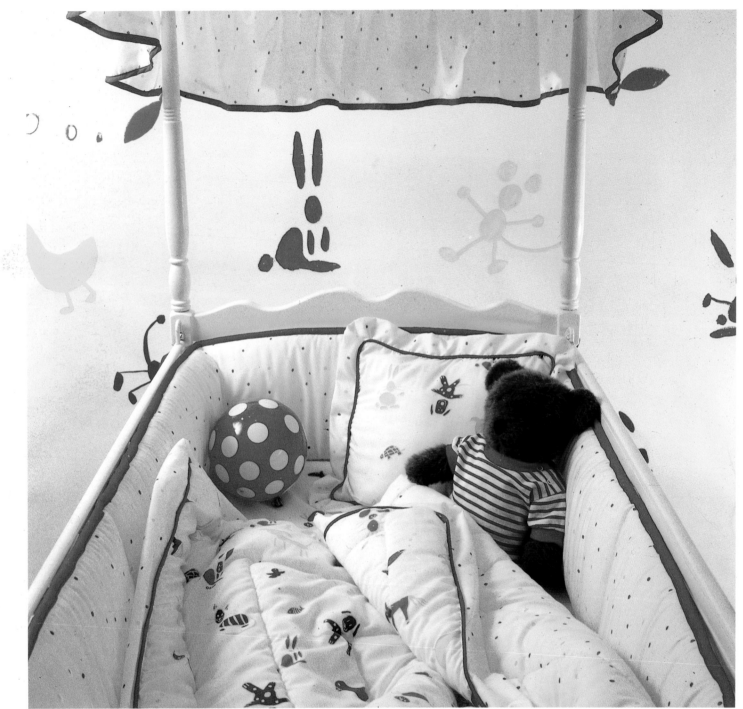

LINEN SET BY GEAR KIDS

BABYWORKS

LINEN SET BY GEAR KIDS

EUROPEAN DOWN COMFORTER BY THE COMPANY STORE

Stave off the dampness of a winter chill with **The Company Store's European Down Comforter.** The classic channel down crib-sized comforter features detailed top-to-bottom stitching with nine ounces of European (goose and duck) down filling the channels in between. Available in pink, light blue, or beige, the comforter is machine washable.

A genuine **Lambskin Comforter** from **Snugli** offers the best in quality construction and easy care. Relaxing and pleasing to a tender touch, lambskin will keep your baby cool in the summer months and warm in the winter months. Whether you use it in the car or infant seat, the crib, the stroller, or the play yard, a Snugli lambskin comforter provides indestructible comfort for the baby. It's nontoxic, sanitized, flame resistant, and machine washable.

PARENTS ADVISE

Lambskin helps babies sleep and helps soothe babies with colic.—KMF

LAMBSKIN COMFORTER BY SNUGLI

For a touch of class at bath time, try **Baby Dior's** 100 percent cotton **Bath Set** that comes with two hooded towels and two baby washcloths. Sporting the Dior label, these soft and absorbent sets will be gentle against your baby's tender skin. They are available with pink or blue trim.

Le Bebe Changing Pad is always ready, even if you're not. Great for busy mothers, the pad is convenient because it folds small enough to fit into a handbag. The softness of this adorable pad soothes baby—making changing time a pleasure. It's durable enough to withstand many washings. Available in pink or blue hearts from **C.B. Dumont and Co.**

Christmas Dinner Bibs by **Silhouettes** give your baby an adorable and festive touch at holiday meals. These catchall bibs are practical as well as cheerful. Your baby will delight in the bright colors, and you'll appreciate the protection the extrawide bibs provide against dribbles and spills.

BATH SET BY BABY DIOR

CHRISTMAS DINNER BIBS BY SILHOUETTE

3

ROCK-A-BYE BABY

SLEEPING AND RESTING

CRIBS AND BASSINETS

Whether it's naptime or lights out for the night, every parent wants to know that baby is safe, secure, and comfortable. A baby's sleeping quarters, from a dresser drawer for the first few weeks of life to a fully equipped bassinet or a goldplated crib, should provide the safety features and the snugness necessary for a peaceful night's sleep.

During the first weeks, bassinets or cradles are often used instead of cribs. Sometimes, babies prefer the closeness and security of the smaller space. Some bassinets can also double as portable cribs. For visits to grandmother's house or the homes of neighbors and friends, a portable crib or carry bed will provide a handy, lightweight sleeping space for the baby. No more lugging around heavy equipment that's often too big to fit in the trunk of the car. With portable cribs, packing up is fast and easy, and you will be assured that your baby will get the rest he needs.

WHAT TO LOOK FOR WHEN CHOOSING A CRIB

- Make sure there's no more than 2⅜ inches (a three-finger width) between the slats of the crib.
- Locks on drop sides should be secured.
- There should be no exposed sharp edges or pinch points to injure a baby's tiny hands.
- There should be less than a two-finger distance between the mattress and the sides of the crib.
- Look for sturdy construction and strong joints.
- Make sure dowels or knobs can't be pulled off.
- If repainting an older crib, use nontoxic paint that won't chip or fade.
- All cribs should meet the safety standards set by federal regulations.

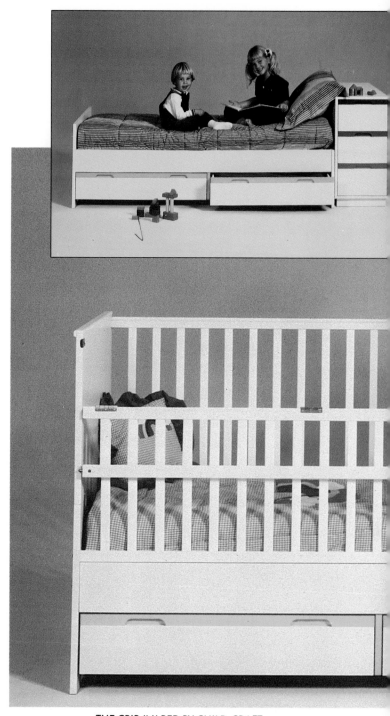

THE CRIB 'N' BED BY CHILD CRAFT

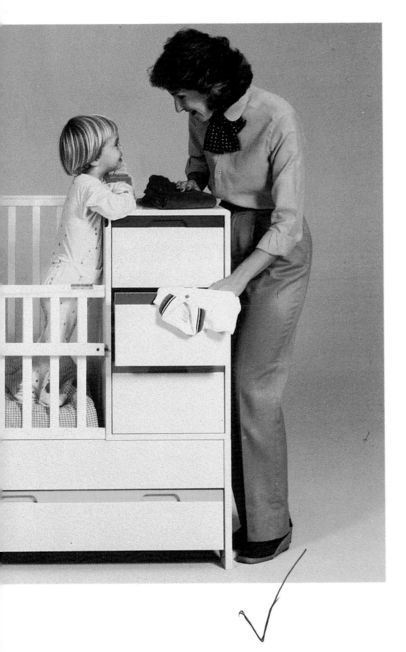

CHILD CRAFT

Each **Child Craft** crib lends a special quality to whatever design theme you choose for the nursery. The fresh new looks will add style as well as practicality to your growing baby's sleeping quarters.

The **Crib 'n' Bed** with rainbow trim is nursery furniture that works for you. It safely confines your baby, but gives him or her freedom and room to grow. Future comfort is assured: simply remove the side rails when the baby outgrows the crib and, *voila!* the entire crib turns into your child's first youth bed. Parents will adore the extra storage space built into the frame and headboard with convenient, recessed handles on the drawers. This crib is available with rainbow trim in either white or natural wood.

Bring the timeless beauty of wood into your child's nursery with the **Country Oak Crib.** All the natural markings and grains are preserved, adding a lovely texture to your baby's living quarters. The ends of the headboard and footboard are gracefully curved, and the side panels can be raised or lowered with the touch of a toe. Casters make moving the crib a snap, allowing for easy cleaning. The crib features four adjustable mattress heights.

Clean, simple lines accentuate the natural-wood **Storybook Crib,** creating the perfect fairy-tale setting for your newborn. The Storybook converts into a four-poster canopy crib, offering parents more than one way to style their nursery. Flounced coverlets accentuate the gracefully curved, Colonial-style canopy frame. The mattress features four adjustable heights, and the double drop sides are easily and conveniently raised or lowered. The Storybook is a warm, livable crib that can be adapted to your own nursery style.

PARENTS ADVISE

Convertible-level portable cribs are great because you can use them both as a play pen at the lowest level and as a crib.— CG

THE DOLLY MADISON ENSEMBLE BY CHILD CRAFT

THE STORYBOOK CRIB BY CHILD CRAFT

Created for today's baby, the **Dolly Madison Crib** is designed with yesterday's stunning attention to detail. On all four sides, each slat is doweled instead of flat, and the scalloped edging at the base of the footboard is gently curved. The crib is both practical and pleasing, combining Colonial styling and quality construction with a mattress that features four convenient adjustable heights. The Dolly Madison is a charming addition to any baby's nursery.

PARENTS ADVISE

If you're buying a secondhand crib, make sure it meets all the federal safety standards. If you're repainting an older crib, use nontoxic paint that won't get discolored.—HB

LEWIS OF LONDON

Baby Cribs from **Lewis of London** have been designed exclusively for the Lewis of London collection and are built by European craftsmen from the finest materials and resources. The distinctive style of each piece brings an atmosphere that's both fashionable and practical to your baby's nursery. The Lewis of London crib will welcome your child with warmth, irresistable·comfort, and a special look and quality all its own.

The **Solange Gold-Plated Crib,** built by Italian craftsmen exclusively for Lewis of London, will provide your baby with endless nights of luxurious repose. The lines and exquisite curves of the headboard and footboard are classics, crafted with a masterful attention to the design. But even this elegant sleeping quarters takes into account the practical needs of you and your baby. The double drop sides glide quietly and smoothly, but lock securely into place once they're adjusted. The mattress features three separate heights to accommodate your child's rapid growth in the first year. Casters make the crib easy to move, and, therefore, easy to clean around. The crib is also available colored in nontoxic white paint that will not chip or fade.

The **Nathalie Crib** (see p. 134) features three looks in one. Remove one side and the crib turns into a charming love seat capable of holding two adults. Remove both side rails and you've just created your child's first youth bed. This versatile piece also features three mattress heights and more than enough storage space below for extra sheets and blankets. The Nathalie Crib is sturdily constructed of beechwood and is available in white and yellow, white and navy, white and red, all natural, and natural and brown.

One of the most functional, versatile, and solidly built cribs of all is **Lewis of London's Baby Block** (see p. 139, also). This finely crafted piece gives new meaning to the word "crib." In addition to the crib, the entire unit contains two night tables with five drawers on each end, two roomy storage drawers at the bottom of the crib, two bookshelves, and a changing table. If that's not enough, the Baby Block also converts into a full-sized European twin bed, and can be used into your child's early school years. It's available in white and red, white and yellow, white and navy, and natural and brown.

The unusual design of the **Lover Crib** makes it a unique addition to a special baby's nursery. There are no true sides, no front or back, to the lover crib. Instead, the ends are

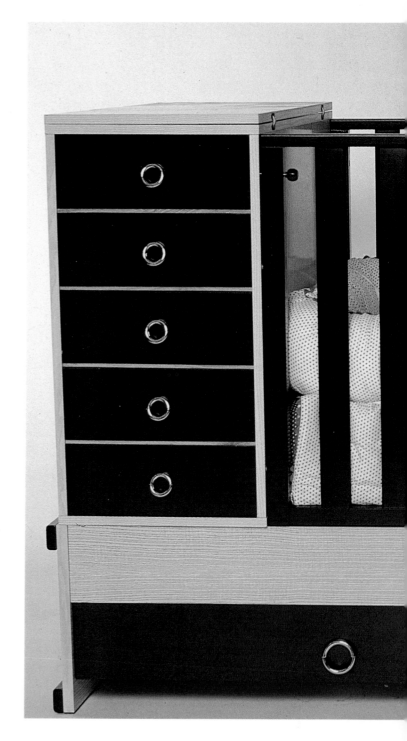

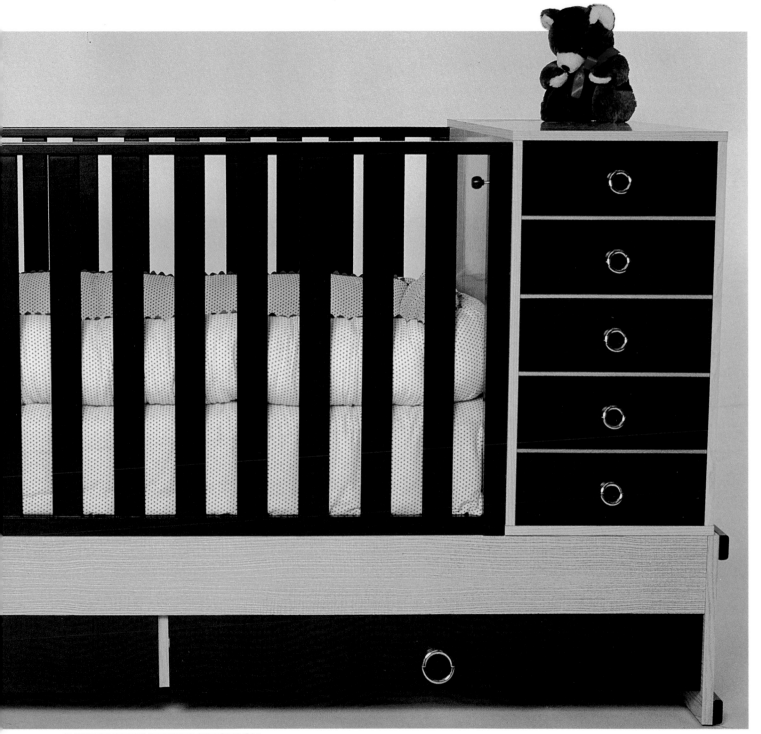

THE BABY BLOCK BY LEWIS OF LONDON

THE LOVER CRIB BY LEWIS OF LONDON

bowed and seem to lovingly embrace the two "side" pieces. The crib can be changed into a youth bed, but it is suggested, for the sake of extra support, that you remove only one "side" when you use it this way. The crib is on casters, has a handy storage drawer below and the mattress has three heights. It is available exclusively at **Lewis of London** in either all natural or all white. No teething bars are necessary on any Lewis of London crib; any paint that is used is baked in, nontoxic, and won't chip or fade.

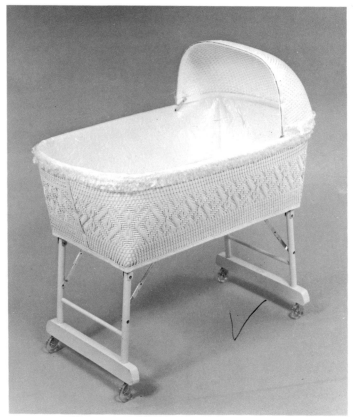

BASSINET BY BADGER

PARENTS ADVISE

Teething bars sometimes crack and may pinch or puncture baby's lips or gums. Lewis of London cribs don't require them.—ELK

BASSINETS AND CRADLES

A bassinet or cradle is often a baby's first bed, offering your newborn the coziness and security of a smaller space. They're charming additions to a nursery, reminiscent of a much more delicate, gentler time for babies.

A standard style **Bassinet** by **Badger** comes with a jumbo-sized basket, making it a longer lasting bed for your newborn. Finely constructed of delicate white wicker, this bassinet can be elegantly dressed with a lacy, flounced coverlet and hood. Wheels at the bottom of the stand make it easy to move from room to room.

Strollee's Deluxe Portable Bassinet is convenient, compact, and easy to carry on visits or trips. The entire bassinet folds by releasing the safety latch. A sturdy steel frame features adjustable heights to prevent unnecessary back

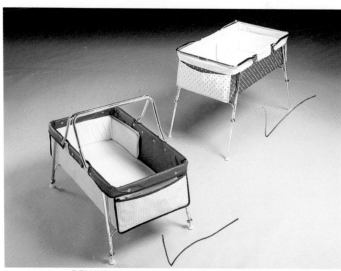

DELUXE PORTABLE BASSINET BY STROLLEE

strain while adults bend over. The padded vinyl interior is comfortable and easily wipes clean. This bassinet, available in a variety of colors, certainly makes a mother's busy life a lot less hectic.

Imported from Italy, the **Reve Bassinet** comes fully dressed and is so comfortable your baby won't be able to resist nestling into it. The stand is elegantly poised, holding a most precious bundle of joy on top. But this stylish bassinet goes beyond an attractive look. It's functional, as well as beautiful. The bed is removable, converting into a convenient carry basket. The casters at the base of the stand are optional.

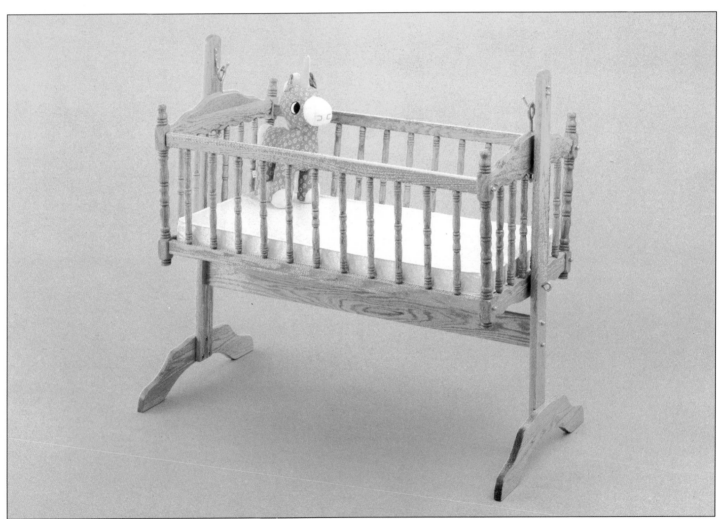

WOODEN CRADLE BY CONNER FOREST INDUSTRIES

During those first few months of life, newborns enjoy the closeness and security of a well-defined space. **Wooden Cradles** by **Conner Forest Industries** offer that sense of security, but with a touch of old-world charm. Finely crafted with gracefully doweled sides, the cradle rocks gently.

The **Brass Bed Company of America** makes **Cradles,** too. For a baby born with a silver spoon in his mouth, a brass cradle is the obvious next step. With elegance, grace, and a richness all its own, the cradle also has a coziness about it and an easy, rocking motion that will make your baby feel very special indeed.

For mothers who spend a good deal of time visiting neighbors and relatives, or traveling back and forth to the babysitter, the **Snugli Carry Bed** will be worth its weight in gold. This lightweight, durable portable bed is convenient to pack and easy to set up. The sides are mesh so your baby can look outside and feel a part of the action, and they zip down easily. The base of the Carry Bed is padded foam for your baby's comfort.

A **Moses Basket** (newly dubbed "William's Basket," after the British royal couple's first happy arrival), offers both charm and elegance in a convenient temporary bed for baby.

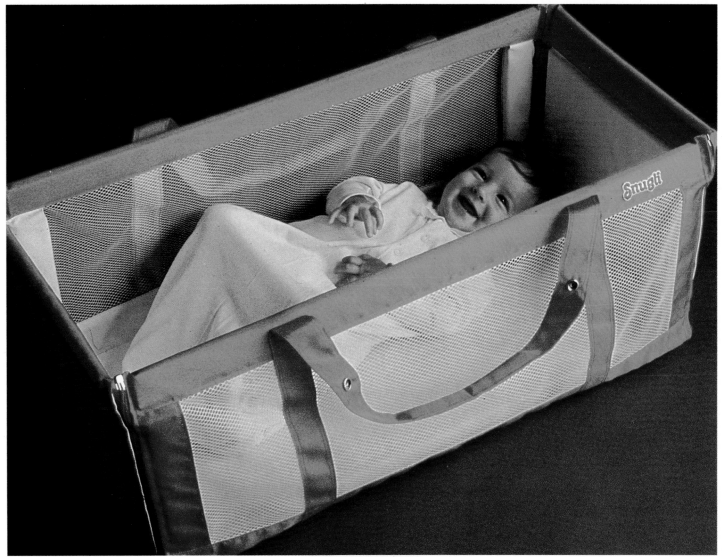

CARRY BED BY SNUGLI

MOSES BASKET BY C.B. DUMONT AND CO.

The wicker basket is about sixteen inches wide and thirty-two inches long, and can be beautifully decorated with a frilly skirt and canopy, a mattress cover, and a blanket. A matching pillow, which should be used only for decoration with babies this age, is also available, all from C. B. Dumont and Co.

The **Evelyn Portacrib,** available exclusively at **Lewis of London**, is the sturdiest portable crib on the market. It's solidly and elegantly constructed of beechwood, so there's no wobbling and, therefore, no worrying about your baby's safety. It features three separate heights, and the crib conveniently folds lengthwise. It is available in natural or white.

The **Paris Portacrib** from the **Paris Maine Corporation** folds in the middle and features two mattress heights. It's lightweight, but durable. The double drop sides can be easily locked into place and wheels at the bottom of the legs make it easy to move.

PARIS PORTACRIB BY THE PARIS MAINE CORP.

INFANT SEATS

Infant seats are great for giving both mom and baby a rest in the middle of a hectic day. The gentle rocking of the seat is enjoyable and soothing for the baby. The seats should be sturdy, but lightweight, so you can conveniently carry the baby with you from room to room.

THINGS TO REMEMBER ABOUT INFANT SEATS

- Make sure the base of the seat splays out wider than the seat itself.
- Look for sturdy construction. The baby should not be able to tip the seat over.
- If you use the seat on the kitchen table or other surfaces above the floor, use clamps to secure the seat.
- Make sure there are no exposed sharp edges and that the safety belt cannot be undone.
- Once a baby can climb out, you should no longer use the seat.

The **Kanga-Rocka-Roo** by **Century** is a versatile seat that's safe and enjoyable for your baby and convenient for you. It can be used as a carry cradle, a rocking seat, or a feeding seat. There's a blue "tech pouch" tucked away beneath for keeping extra baby bottles and supplies handy. The seat is solidly constructed of sturdy molded plastic and comes in either bright yellow or beige with a comfortable vinyl insert or sheepskin coverlet. The sheepskin keeps the baby warm in the winter, but cool in the summer.

The **Baby Bjorn** is a lightweight, simply designed, bouncing **Infant Seat** that will give your baby hours of enjoyment and soothing relaxation. Made of 100 percent cotton stretched onto a sturdy metal frame, it gently conforms to your baby's shape. The baby slips into the fabric saddle and is securely, comfortably buckled in by the safety belt. Baby Bjorn is available in bright primary or pastel colored fabric, or seersucker, any of which will stimulate your newborn's senses of sight and touch. There's also a toy rod with colorful wooden play beads to keep your baby entertained.

KANGA-ROCKA-ROO BY CENTURY

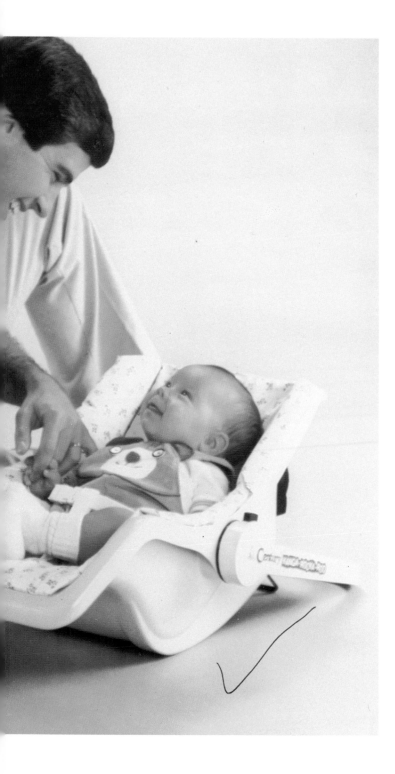

INFANT SEAT BY BABY BJORN

R O C K E R S

Rock-a-Bye Baby! The **Boston Rocker** (see p. 133) is an American classic you and your child will treasure for a lifetime. Solidly constructed by **U.S. Furniture Industries**, the rocker has a simply curved seat and a spindled back. The narrow softly pointed rockers give a quiet, soothing ride that won't wake your sleeping baby, and the armrests are traditionally curved at a comfortable height.

The traditional markings of natural wood have been adapted into a contemporary look in a modern-style **Rocker** by **U.S. Furniture Industries**. The seat is roomy and the back is contoured to conform to your own shape. The chair is sturdy, rocks quietly, and is adaptable to any nursery setting.

4

CLOTHES ENCOUNTERS

Comfort, quality construction and design, and easy-care instructions are top priorities when purchasing clothing for your children. Any item you choose should take into account your baby's rapid growth in these early years and the need for movement and activity.

For infants, you should look for garments that are made from fabrics that are absorbent and that "breathe" such as lightweight cottons and knits. During this busy time, clothes that are washable and allow for easy diaper changes will be advantageous to you. You should also avoid elastics and tight knits that bind, and remember that babies usually prefer clothing that doesn't pull on over their heads.

What size your baby wears should be determined by weight instead of age. There are always exceptions, but the chart below will give some beginning guidelines to help in your selection. The clothing featured in this chapter is available in the sizes, or in the equivalent of the sizes, listed in the chart below.

SIZE	WEIGHT
Newborn	Birth to 5½ lbs.
3 months	up to 13 lbs.
6 months	up to 18 lbs.
12 months	up to 22 lbs.
18 months	up to 25 lbs.

Built-in growth features are a plus for children at any age or weight. Items with adjustable straps, grow tucks, elastic inserts, or undefined waistlines last longer and provide a better fit for the growing child. Clothing with zippers and openings that are easy to work will eventually encourage a child to learn to dress himself.

Babies usually don't care how they look as long as they're warm and comfortable, but, as the child gets older, he or she will begin to show increasing concern about appearances. Clothing can have quite a bit of influence on a child's emotions and sense of self. It's important that children like what they're wearing. Children between 12 and 18 months of age are just beginning to establish a sense of self-confidence and independence. The clothing they wear should be a reflection of their own individual personalities, but shouldn't set them too far apart from other children.

WHAT TO LOOK FOR WHEN SELECTING CLOTHING

- Look for sturdy construction. Check for reinforced seams and knees, double-stitched armholes and neck and pocket edges, and resilient elastic.
- Buttons, hooks, or snaps should be firmly attached.
- Look for growth features such as adjustable straps, grow tucks, snap crotches, undefined waistlines, and enough fullness in armholes and seat.
- Bright colors stimulate infants, and eventually, help to teach children—"red" pants, "blue" coat, etc. Bright colors also alert motorists to a child's presence on the street.
- Look for the proper fit. Make sure clothes hang from the shoulders instead of the neck.
- Make sure clothes don't rub, bag, or bind, causing discomfort.
- Shirts and blouses should be long enough to stay tucked in.
- Snowsuits should be big enough to fit over other clothes comfortably.
- Clothes that are washable and don't require ironing are convenient and economical.

PARENTS ADVISE

I've found that the more clothing you have on hand—especially underwear items for the baby—the less frequently you have to do laundry.—SC

AT HOME

Changing clothes about five or six times a day is not an uncommon part of a baby's everyday routine. Stretchies, t-shirts, baby gowns, and body suits are often worn around-the-clock in a baby's early years. Babies need clothing that's going to last and clothing that's comfortable and absorbent, but there are no rules that say it can't be fashionable, too.

Petit Bateau's hooded **Baby Gowns** rate high in hugability. The endearing softness of these 100 percent cotton

BABY GOWNS AND STRETCHIES BY PETIT BATEAU

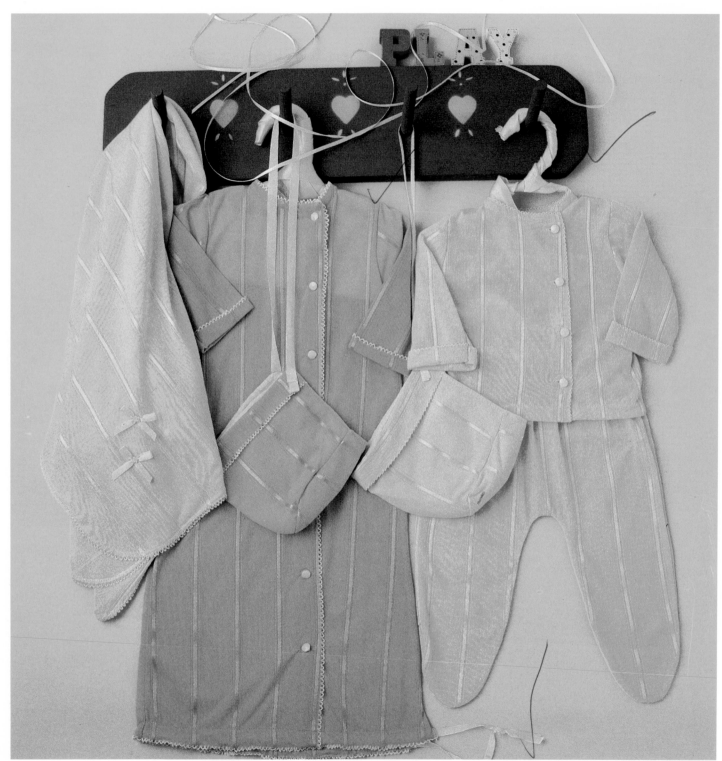

BABY GOWN AND BONNET SETS BY SHEPHERD MANUFACTURING

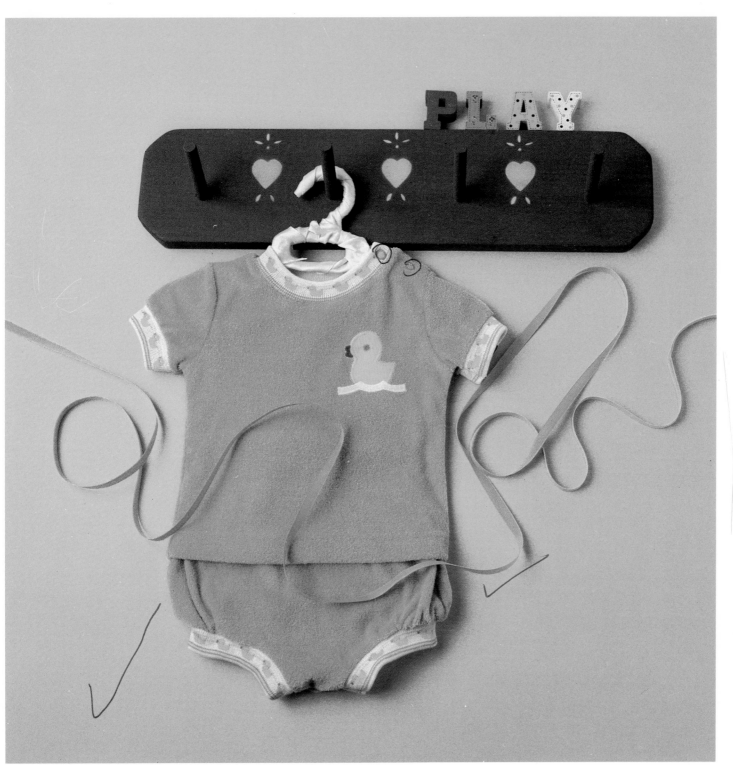

DIAPER SUIT BY SYLVIA WHYTE

durable and comfortable, providing all-purpose activewear for babies. Sweaters and pram suits are a must for the colder weather.

Your little fashion plate can crawl around in style with **Sylvia Whyte's** two-piece **Creeper** in lightweight baby blue brushed corduroy. It buttons at the shoulders and has an adorable little red-and-blue stitched soldier on the front. A cream colored, lightweight, short-sleeved shirt peeks out from beneath the coverall. This comfy ensemble is great for both playtime and special occasions. Made from a cotton/polyester blend, the creeper is machine washable.

Anchors aweigh! **Sylvia Whyte's Sailor-Style Creeper** is perfect for your little adventurer at playtime, for visiting friends or relatives, or for special occasions like the Fourth of July. This classic outfit has been given an even more appealing look with the shipshape lines of Whyte's blue-and-white pinstripe design with a sailor neckline and blue sailor ties. The creeper is in two pieces with the bottom buttoning to the top clear around the waistline. Made from a cotton/polyester blend, the suit is machine washable.

This **Legging and Sweater Dress Set** by **Petit Bateau** will keep your baby warm and toasty throughout the early fall and winter months. The red sweater dress with a zigzag yellow line pattern is adorned with a royal blue tie and collar, and finished off with royal blue leggings. Your baby, whether a boy or girl, will love the softness, comfort, and security this outfit provides. Although you should initially hand wash the red sweater in cold water, you can machine wash the entire garment from then on. Matching socks and a hat are also available.

Osh Kosh B'Gosh Overalls for babies and toddlers come in so many different styles that they're suitable for playing, parties, shopping trips, or holidays. And these adorable little overalls last forever. Styles include the classic denim, fire-

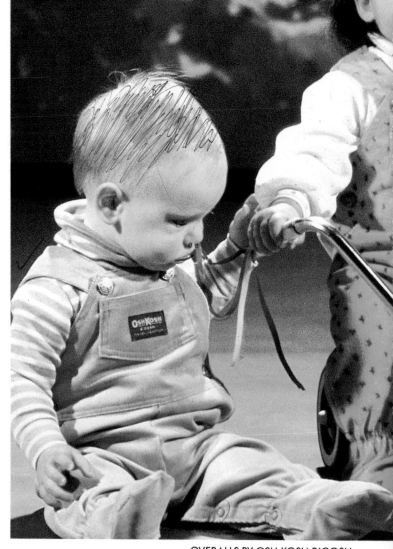

OVERALLS BY OSH KOSH B'GOSH

64

SWEATER SET BY PETIT BATEAU

engine red, hot pink, blue-and-white pinstripe, and much, much more. You can dress them up with a t-shirt, blouse, or baby flannel, or, if the temperature's risin', baby can wear them alone.

PARENTS ADVISE

Besides being adorable, Osh Kosh over-alls have a wider cut which makes them more comfortable to wear over heavy sweaters or with diapers.—ALK

If your little one is about to embark on major repairs of toy trucks and trains, it's only fitting that he or she is dressed for the job. **Marimekko's** tiny auto mechanic **Coveralls** are just the ticket. The long-sleeved suit is made of sturdy blue cotton and has the bright red-orange Marimekko car on the back. Infant sizes are available in 12, 18, and 24 months. Pass the wrench, please.

Babies like to get in shape, too! **Marimekko's Jogging Suits** are ideal for your baby's active lifestyle or maybe for the classes at the Playorena (see p. 107). Even if baby's not up and walking, (or off and running), it's easy to warm up to the soft comfortable cotton suit. It is available in pink or blue in infant sizes 12, 18 or 24 months.

SWEATERS

Snuggle your baby up in a 100 percent wool **Sweater** from **Lamkins**. Hand knit in England, this adorable gray sweater has a red-and-white double-decker British bus on the front with LONDON spelled out in black down the side of the bus. The sweater has long sleeves and a crew neck.

For boys or girls, try a classic **Cable Knit Sweater** by **Florianne**. Made in France of 100 percent wool, the long-sleeved crew neck sweater buttons at the shoulders and is available in a lush green or a deep navy blue. You can find this sweater at Au Chat Botte.

Also from France, by **Ozona,** is an elegant **Cardigan Sweater** for little girls. The V-neck is exquisite, and the natural shade is a classic. The sweater is made from washable acrylic that won't irritate your baby's tender skin.

CARDIGAN SWEATER BY OZONA

SWIMWEAR

New York designer Sharon Barnett Miskit and her partner Bunny Roma Hart have placed the emphasis on style and distinction in their line of sexy little swimsuits for babies. More accurately called **Diaper Suits** (they're cut wide to cover baby's entire diapered bottom), the new designs offer comfort and class. In "The Garbo," "The Marilyn", or "The One-Shoulder Jane," a combination of mystery and innocence is barely emphasized, yet subtly apparent. Babies will look wild in "The Tarzan," dazzling in "The Tuxedo Suit," or simply humble and lovable in "The Super-Baby Maillot." For more information about these great suits, contact Bunny Roma Hart at Unique, 1333 Broadway, Room 1107 in New York City.

Marimekko combines splash and dash in its latest **Swimwear** for your chic little beach bum. Flashy pink-and-white or blue-and-white striped tank suits are for girls, and swim trunks in the same colors for boys. The tank suits are made from a cotton/lycra blend and the boys' trunks from 100 percent cotton. With those shades and sand pail and shovel, yours will be the grooviest baby on the beach.

SNOWSUITS

For those cold winter days, make your choice of snowsuits practical and stylish with this dusty-pink-and-gray two-piece **Snowsuit** by **Creation Stummer.** The inside stuffing is thick with a tough but gentle-to-the-touch cotton/polyester exterior. The hood buttons to the collar, so it is removable on warmer winter days. Pink-and-grey pipings accent the hood, cuffs, and zipper front.

Your baby will be toasty warm but super cool in this one-piece **Snowsuit** by **Mini Robin,** of the **Robin Sportswear's**

◆◆◆◆◆◆◆◆◆◆◆◆◆◆◆◆◆◆◆◆◆◆◆◆◆◆◆◆

PARENTS ADVISE

It's often a good idea to monogram your baby's clothing so it won't get lost, especially at a day-care center or during a visit with friends or neighbors.—LF

◆◆◆◆◆◆◆◆◆◆◆◆◆◆◆◆◆◆◆◆◆◆◆◆◆◆◆◆

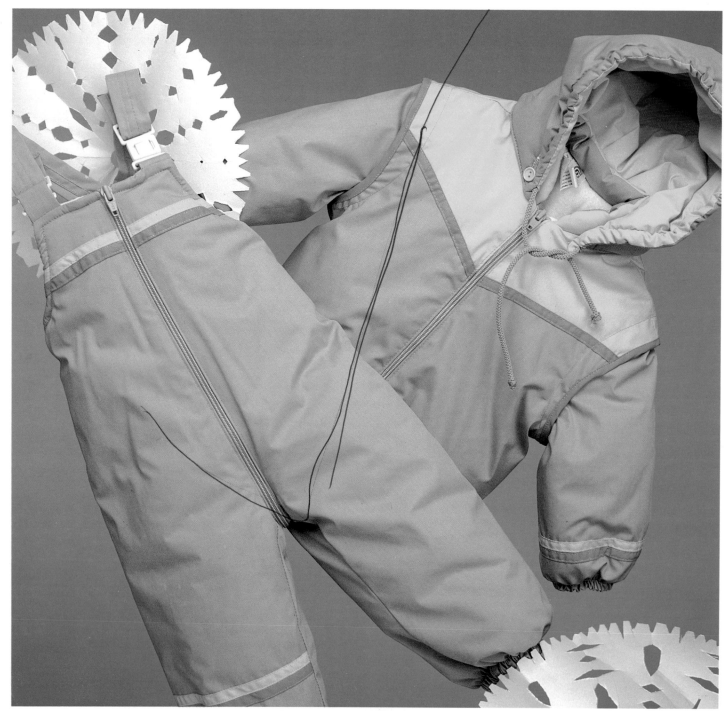

SNOWSUIT BY CREATION STUMMER

Designer Collection of Montreal, Quebec. A zipper conveniently extends from the neck to the leg of this light pink, blue, and cream-colored suit in stylish Grand Prix fabric. The suit is slightly gathered in the middle with an elastic insert for a more tailored look. The tie-hood and rib-knit cuffs on the arms and legs keep out nasty drafts. The lining is nylon filled with nine ounces of holocord stuffing, and the exterior is a cotton/polyester blend. This is a snazzy suit for babies already living in the fast pram lane.

SPECIAL OCCASIONS

Your baby's first parties and holidays are special times shared by the whole family. The cameras will no doubt be clicking away, trying to capture your little boy in his finest suit jacket or your little girl in her best dress. The following selections are especially suited for your baby's first social engagements, so she'll look fashionable from the start.

CHRISTENING GOWNS

The finest in European fashions has been adapted for affordable **Christening Gowns** for boys and girls by **Mothercare Stores.** Each is exclusively styled, featuring elaborate lacework, elegant linings, and beautiful petticoats. Outfits for boys come in either one- or two-piece shorts-and-top sets with adorable Peter Pan collars. Matching hats or christening bonnets are included and bibs, coordinated for the total look, are also available. Made of 100 percent cotton or of a cotton/polyester blend, the christening outfits are machine washable.

Saks Fifth Avenue features a superb collection of individually designed **Christening Gowns** for boys and girls. No two gowns are alike and each one is designed and brilliantly executed by the hands of craftsmen. The detailed lacework, elaborate petticoats, and fine fabrics are especially suited for the treasured event.

PARTY CLOTHES

An elegant **Challis Dress** by **Babetta** features a finely crafted hand-smocked bodice that's high off the waist, so it doesn't bind. Beauty, comfort, and style make this charming dress especially suited for special occasions. It buttons behind the neck and ties in back. There's a dainty petticoat beneath, adding to the old-fashioned charm of the garment. Imported from Italy, the dress is available at Botticellinos in a light pink or cream.

Christian Dior's Shorts and Jacket Outfit is a trim combination perfect for your little boy's first parties and special outings. The soft, feltlike suspender shorts have adjustable buttons. A tiny gray-and-black glen plaid lapelless jacket sports the Dior label and there's a separate white short-sleeved shirt beneath the shorts. Made of a cotton/polyester blend, the outfit is also available with a red jacket and black velvet shorts. For little sisters, there's a matching gray-and-black glen plaid dress with a white bodice and lace border, also with the Dior label subtly stitched white on white. Both outfits are available in 18 months size and older.

Envision your daughter in the incomparable elegance of a **Dress** from **Christian Dior's Enfant Collection.** A high Victorian collar and narrow cuffs are adorned with white lacework that spills over the neckline to create the bodice. Made of a cotton/acetate blend, the entire dress has a white luster heightened by accents of a tiny red rosebud at the base of the neck and a striking red satin sash. The torso is elongated, pouring into a 1920s-style dropped waistline. It is available in sizes for 12 months and older.

Also from **Christian Dior's Enfant Collection** is this stylish black polka-dot **Party Dress.** The black-on-white dress is accented with a red rosebud at the base of the white Peter Pan collar. A black velvet bodice has a rounded scalloped edge complementing the dotted pattern of the skirt and long sleeves. The permanent-press dress is 100 percent polyester for easy care and convenience. It comes in 18 months size and older.

The soft colors and simple lines of **Sylvia Whyte's Brother and Sister Apparel** let the sweetness and playful charm of your child's personality shine through. A light pink, polished cotton dress for your little girl, with a complimentary piece for a little boy, is perfect for both special and informal occasions. It endearing features include a white ruffled bib front with a delicate rosebud at the neck and dainty, puffed short sleeves.

BROTHER AND SISTER APPAREL BY SYLVIA WHYTE

BABYWORKS

PINK DRESS BY SYLVIA WHYTE

The bib ties in the back and is easily removed for no-hassle care. The material is actually a cotton/polyester blend and is conveniently washable.

The old-world elegance of Little Lord Fauntleroy has been adapted to a contemporary look of richness and sophistication in **Magil's Knickers** for little boys. A long-sleeved black velvet blouson with a ruffled front bib buttons onto the black-and-gray checked knickers. Knickers and bib are made of 100 percent wool woven in Scotland. A white Peter Pan collar has a deep gray velvet bow tie at the neck. The buttons on the knickers are adjustable, and there are tucks that can be let out or taken in to accommodate your child. The same outfit is available for little girls with a matching gray-and-black checked skirt, instead of the knickers. It is imported from Italy in sizes for 12 months and older, but is available at Botticellino's.

BABY SHOES

"Look at me, I'm walking!" The time for your baby's first pair of shoes has come when the child is able to pull herself up and take that big first step. Baby shoes are the one item you shouldn't buy "cheap." It's important to get a good-quality shoe that fits properly in order to avoid discomfort or serious problems with you child's feet later on.

Some parents have their babies wearing pre-walker shoes during the first six months. These shoes, although they may look nice, are not really necessary, because babies usually can't stand up at this time. If you do decide to use prewalkers, make sure you get a perfect fit. During this time, the bones in your baby's feet are most tender .

When the time comes for buying shoes, make sure the salesperson you have is experienced in fitting shoes. There should be at least ½ inch between your baby's toe and the end of the shoe. Make sure the baby toe and big toe do not rub

uncomfortably against the sides of the shoe and that the heel does not slip when your baby walks.

Shoes are necessary for keeping your child's feet warm and dry. They also protect feet from tacks, splinters, or other sharp objects you may not be able to detect ahead of time. Flat, wide-bottom baby shoes help your new little explorer balance. Also, it's a good idea to have more than one pair of shoes on hand and not to wait too long before buying a new pair; baby feet grow very quickly.

CAREFUL CONSIDERATIONS IN SHOE SELECTION

- Make sure the sole is flexible. It should bend at the ball of the foot as the baby walks.
- Flat leather soles are more flexible than rubber soles.
- Flatness helps baby balance and helps prevent rolling inward or outward.
- The back of the shoe should be sturdy, not squishy, to prevent baby's heel from slipping.
- A slight heel in shoe is necessary for sufficient support.
- The top side of shoe should also be flexible, with enough room to give when baby bends its foot.
- Make sure there's enough room for baby's toes. If the littlest toe is pressing up against the edge of the shoe, then the shoe is too tight.
- White cotton socks are best to wear with shoes, because they're the most absorbent. Make sure there's room in the sock as well as the shoe. Fold the excess sock over the top of foot, not the bottom.
- Canvas or nylon shoes do not breathe as well as leather ones.
- Three-quarter high-tops help keep your baby's shoe on the foot, while providing more room for growth and ankle movement than the higher, more traditional length high-top.
- Soft surfaces, such as shag rugs and cushions, are difficult for baby to walk on.

Botticellino's features a special collection of the very best **Leather Shoes** for babies and toddlers. Made in Italy, these shoes sport a style and fit that cannot be found in any other

RUNNING SHOES BY NIKE

baby shoe store. Whether it's for school, playtime, or special occasions, Botticellinos will always have the shoe that's especially suited to your child's individual needs and personality. From the more rugged high-top red leather boot to the dainty, chic little party shoe, the entire line is well-designed by quality craftsmen from the finest materials.

For your newest little tenderfoot, try **Marimekko's** genuine leather **Moccasins.** Their natural contour fit won't manipulate or restrict your baby's foot. They're easy to put on, but snug enough so they won't fall off. The moccasins are handmade in the United States by Sven Design in San Francisco. They're great for both indoor and outdoor activity, and are available in red, beige, dark brown, or gray.

Off and running. **Nike** now makes **"Running" Shoes** especially suited for infants. The front of the shoes are wider and deeper than some sneakers to help babies balance. The soles are flexible and treaded for a good grip on soft carpets or smooth surfaces. They're available in a variety of styles including the multicolored "Tabby," the sleek "Tyro," and the "Romp" for the extremely ambitious baby.

5

TAKING CARE

FEEDING AND BATHING

FEEDING

Feeding time is a special, enjoyable experience that strengthens the bond between a baby and parents. Before you begin feeding, you should get into a comfortable position. If you're bottle feeding, use a pillow or cushion to support your arm. Cradle the baby in the crook of your arm in a semireclining position. Hold the baby about twelve inches away, so you can look at each other. Soothe the baby with the gentle sounds of your voice.

If you're breast feeding, you may want to pad the inside of your brassiere to absorb any leaking milk. A nursing pad, or soft cloth diaper underneath the baby's chin also helps to catch dribbles. It's a good idea to keep a few relief bottles on hand and a few extra nursing bras, as well. If you do decide to breast feed, once your baby starts on solid foods, you can hand express your milk for mixing into cereals and other foods.

When bottle feeding, the formula should fill the nipple to prevent the baby from swallowing too much air. Don't insist on feeding her or him the whole bottle. Remember that sucking takes a lot of energy, so sometimes babies need to stop to take a rest.

Remember never to put a baby to bed with a bottle, because doing so may cause tooth decay. Sugar from formula or juice cannot be rinsed away by a sleeping baby's saliva. After every feeding, wipe an infant's gums and teeth with a soft, clean washcloth or gauze pad.

SCHEDULES

Because each baby's appetite is different, the amount and frequency of feedings vary, too. Babies under six months old require about fifty-five calories per ounce, so babies, during this time, will drink two-and-a-half to three ounces a day for every pound they weigh. In general, babies get hungry again three to four hours after a feeding.

BABY'S WEIGHT	AMOUNT OF FORMULA
6lbs.	15oz. a day
8	20
10	25
12	30

BOTTLES

Whether you decide to breast feed or bottle feed your baby, you're going to need bottles. For breast-feeding mothers, three should be enough. You'll need them as relief bottles for extra formula, juice, or water. If bottle feeding, you should have eight bottles, with nipples, collars, and caps to fit.

Bottles are either plastic or glass. Plastic is safer and lighter, making the bottles more suitable for travel or for toddlers who can hold their own bottles. Glass bottles weather sterilization better and are more appropriate for a newborn. They don't get scratched and it's easier to read the amounts.

Instead of bottles, you may want to consider nursers which hold formula in sterilized disposable bags. You use them once, then throw them away. Although a little more expensive than bottles, nursers keep the baby from sucking in too much air while drinking. Nipples for nursers usually need to be of the same brand in order to fit, whereas a variety of nipples will do the trick on bottles. When a nipple starts to show signs of wear and tear, replace it with a new one. It's a good idea to keep extras handy anyway.

PREPARING BOTTLES
What You'll Need
- Pitcher or measuring cup
- Can opener
- Sterilizing kit with a rack for holding bottles, or a deep pot
- Funnel
- Long spoon for stirring
- Measuring spoons
- Bottle warmer

The best idea is to get all the bottles you'll need for the day ready at one time. Before you begin, make sure you wash all the nipples, caps, collars, and bottles in soapy water and let them stand to dry. Pour boiling water over the top of the formula can to clean it before opening. The can opener, too, should be cleaned in this way.

Next, mix the formula according to the instructions the doctors will give you. Then, pour the formula into the bottles with the help of a funnel. Place the nipples upside down and gently screw on the caps. Make sure the caps are not on too tight, or steam will get trapped inside. Fill your pot or sterilizer with three to four inches of water and boil the bottles for twenty-five minutes. Let the bottles cool, tighten the caps, and pop them into the refrigerator to use later.

When it's feeding time, warm the bottles with a bottle warmer or simply place them in a pan of warm water for a few minutes; make sure it's not too hot, just lukewarm.

Evenflo makes both **Glass** and **Plastic Bottles** in four- and eight-ounce sizes. Plastic bottles are available clear and in colors to brighten up feeding time. There are four kinds of **Nipples** by Evenflo, also, besides the standard, single hole model. There is a cross-cut opening for heavy formula, thick juices, and cereal; a "blind" nipple that allows you to make your own cut; a "preemie" for babies whose sucking is not so strong; and a "lifetime" style made of more durable material. Evenflo nipples also feature two different shapes. Regular nipples are long and slender, and orthodontic nipples, shaped to the baby's palate are more suited to an infant's proper oral development. Evenflo nipples will fit on any standard bottle.

The **Infa-feeder** is another first-rate **Bottle Feeder.** Infa's feeders are tested by pediatricians and designed with the latest scientific discoveries in mind. Infa's **Pur Nipple,** made from Purelife silicone (a material used in making heart valves), won't crack or discolor and has no odor or taste. It's soft and easy to clean with a guarantee of three years. The Pur nipple fits any standard bottle and is available in both regular and orthodontic shapes.

For the most luxurious of feedings, try the exquisite crystal **Baby Bottle** by **Galway Irish Crystal.** The silver collar and traditional-style nipple add a touch of class to this great gift idea for a very special baby.

Parents Advise

If the nipple's hole is too small, heat a needle and stick it in the rubber. If you make the hole too big, boil the nipple for five minutes to close it.—PL

BABY BOTTLE BY GALWAY IRISH CRYSTAL

THE INFA-FEEDER BOTTLE FEEDER BY MONTEREY LABS

PACIFIERS

You shouldn't be stingy with pacifiers; it's natural for babies to want to suck. Let your baby enjoy at least a little bit of the comfort and security a pacifier provides, especially during those first few scary months of life. Make sure the pacifier won't come apart into pieces that could be swallowed.

The **Nuk Pacifier-Exerciser** from **Reliance Products** is the original orthodontic pacifier and one of the best for your baby's oral development. It's soft and comfortable and shaped in such a way that it helps to properly develop the tiny muscles around a baby's mouth.

PARENTS ADVISE

Some doctors believe that sucking on pacifiers can contribute to weight gain in premature infants.—AJM

SOLID FOODS

Every child is different and there is no set time for an infant to begin eating solid foods. Consult your pediatrician, but watch for any signals that the baby might be sending you. Whenever you do begin to introduce solid foods into a baby's diet, you should do so gradually. Keep an eye out for obvious or sudden changes in bowel movements, a colicky baby, or allergic reactions, signs that baby is not adjusting to solid food well. Start with plain foods that are easily digested, introducing them one at a time and about four or five days apart, so you can keep an eye out for any adverse reactions and know exactly what caused them. Fortified cereal or applesauce is usually good first food for baby, but pay attention to your baby's tastes. You may find he prefers fruits and vegetables over cereal.

Certain foods should be avoided in an infant's diet. Some babies are sensitive to wheat products, certain citrus juices, and egg whites, so these foods are often withheld from a baby's diet until after the first year. It's also a good idea to use only small amounts of salt, sugar, or other spices and seasonings in baby's food.

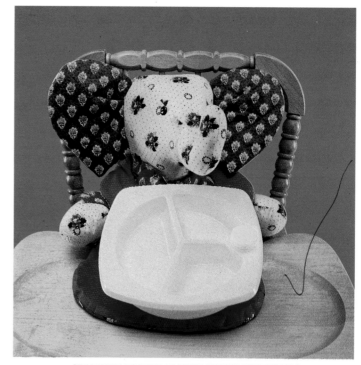

NUK PACIFIER-EXERCISER BY RELIANCE PRODUCTS

STAY WARM FEEDING DISH BY THE FIRST YEARS

Preparing your own baby food is not a formidable task with **The Original Happy Baby Food Grinder.** It's a convenient, easy-to-use hand grinder that helps lower your food costs and provides better nutrition for your baby. Simple in design, the baby food grinder is made from plastic with a stainless steel cutter and swivel handle. Grind up cooked meats, fruits, and vegetables to avoid the high salt and sugar content of many commercial baby foods. The Happy Baby Food Grinder, available from **Bowland-Jacobs International, Incorporated,** is easy to clean and dishwasher safe.

PARENTS ADVISE

I cook and puree meat and vegetables in large quantities. Then I spoon it into ice-cube trays, freeze it, and remove the cubes from the trays. Store them in plastic bags in the freezer and you can use them as you need them.—MAR

DINNERWARE SET AND FLATWARE SET BY THE FIRST YEARS

DISHES

The **Stay Warm Feeding Dish** from **The First Years** will keep your child's food at the same warm temperature throughout the meal. The suction base holds this practical dish in place, preventing any accidental trips off the tray and onto the floor. Dishwasher-safe and unbreakable, the dish has three parts which are easily separated.

Dribbles and spills are a way of life for babies, especially when they're first learning how to eat and drink. The **Tommee Tippee Cup Set** from **Glenco** lends your baby a helping hand and makes cleaning up spills less of a chore for you. Both the four-ounce juice cup and the six-ounce training cup with double-sided handles come with lids especially designed to make drinking easy. The curved, weighted bottoms provide a rocking resistance to prevent major upsets. The cup sets are available in most department stores in a variety of patterns.

Unbreakable Dinnerware Sets are a must for any novice eater. Long-lasting, stain-resistant and dishwasher-safe, the set includes a baby plate, bowl, and cup in brightly colored, assorted decorations. From **The First Years,** they provide practical, convenient, home dining for baby.

The First Years also offers **Flatware Training Sets** made of deluxe stainless steel. The blunt-edged tines on the fork and the deep rounded bowl of the spoon are especially suited for your baby's tender mouth. The handles are wide and easy to grasp. The sets are easy to clean and dishwasher safe.

BIBS

All babies are messy eaters, especially when they're just starting on solid foods. There are basically two types of bibs: teething bibs are small and needed mostly to protect clothing while baby is teething; feeding bibs are large and designed to keep babies from wearing their food. (For messy babies, you might want to try bibs with long sleeves or bibs that reach below the waist.)

Marimekko offers stylish **Feeding Bibs** in red, yellow, or blue stripes. There's nothing smarter to brighten up a baby's feeding time. A clear food catcher on the bottom sees to it that nothing dribbles by. The bibs are plastic, easy to clean, and they tie easily around the baby's neck.

HIGH CHAIRS

When your baby is able to sit up on his own, it's time for a high chair. He'll love being included in the family circle during dinner time—playing or tasting finger foods, and engaging in dinner "conversations." A high chair will keep baby off your lap, and will give you and your baby a whole new outlook on feeding time.

HELPFUL HINTS FOR CHOOSING A HIGH CHAIR

- The high chair should have a wide, sturdy base that won't tip when baby gets restless or too playful.
- Don't put the chair by the stove or electrical outlets and appliances.
- A removable tray is easier to clean, but make sure the tray locks into place securely.
- Always use the safety straps and never leave baby unattended.
- Watch out for small children playing around the baby in a high chair; they may accidentally pull it over.
- Make sure there are no sharp edges or corners exposed that may cause injury.
- Tray should have a lip to catch spills and be wide enough to hold a baby dish.

Fisher Price has designed their **High Chair** especially for messy eaters. The wide wraparound tray tilts spills away from the baby, and raised elbow rests help keep the baby's arms out of the food. Both seat and tray are removable for easy cleaning. The padded vinyl upholstery is covered in fabric that won't crack or tear. Set on a wide-body sturdy frame, the entire chair folds easily for storage and portability. The safety strap holds the baby securely in place. A more traditional-style wooden chair with the same features is also available from Fisher Price.

PARENTS ADVISE

Chopped or cubed fruits, diced, cooked vegetables, and soft cheeses are great finger foods for a baby to start with.—SM

HIGH CHAIR BY FISHER PRICE

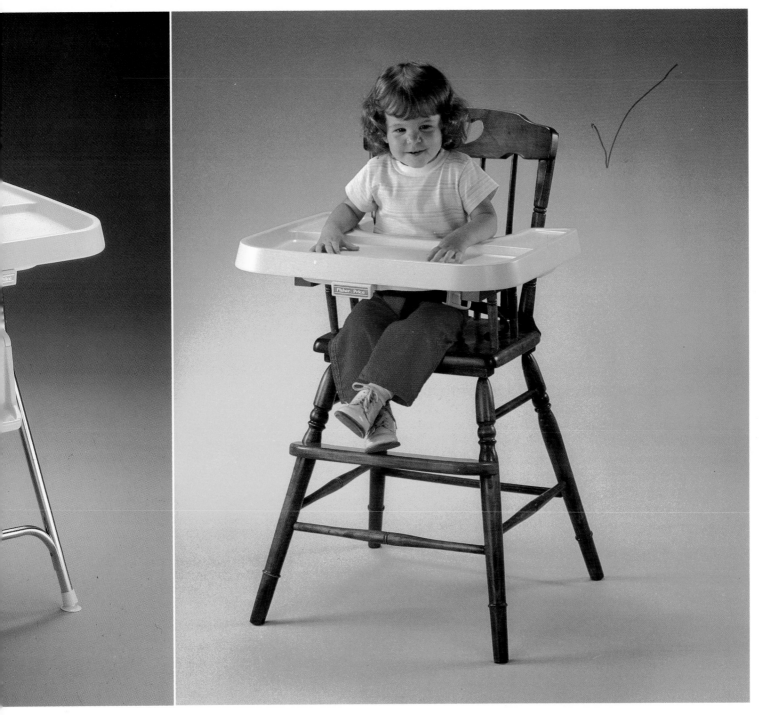

HIGH CHAIR BY FISHER PRICE

Designers working with pediatricians are responsible for the **Brevi Hi-Lo Chair,** which features a padded, contour-fit, high-back seat. An adjustable height makes feeding easier. The tray is dishwasher safe and snaps out for easy cleaning. The wide chrome frame splays out at the base to insure stability, and rollers allow the chair to be easily moved from one room to the other. The Hi-Lo chair is available at Lewis of London.

BATHING

Many babies love bathing right from the start, while others get cranky or are frightened. Always be gentle and soothing—relax, and eventually your baby will too.

Babies require only sponge baths during the first few weeks of life. When the umbilical cord falls off, you should move them to a portable bath or tub. Many parents prefer the portable tub to the regular tub, because they can move it to a comfortable surface height so they don't have to bend over. Also, with a portable tub the baby won't slip around so much.

Although bathing is an important part of a baby's routine, it's not necessary to bathe a child every day. Overbathing will cause chafing and will dry out a baby's delicate skin. A general guideline is to bathe your child about three times a week, but if this seems to be too often, cut down.

Before you begin bathtime, you should have everything you need set up on a tray or in a small layette basket. Here's a handy list of what to have for baby's bath:

BATH SUPPLIES
- Portable bath
- 4 towels, 2 washcloths
- Baby soap and soap dish
- Baby shampoo
- Powder or cornstarch
- Baby oil/lotion/petroleum jelly
- Cotton balls
- Brush and comb set
- After-bath cover-up

Always remember to be gentle when bathing baby, using your fingertips instead of your fingernails to massage baby's head when shampooing. Baby soap and shampoo are milder than regular soap and shampoo, and therefore, gentler on an infant's tender skin.

Gently pat a baby dry. Baby washcloths and towels are softer and easier to use than adult size. Small baby washcloths are more suitable for an infant's tiny ears and bottom. Baby towels are usually hooded so you can cover the head, offering more protection from drafts than adult towels.

You may want to sprinkle powder or cornstarch on the baby to keep him or her dry; if you do, don't shake on too much. Cornstarch is preferred, because there's less danger of a baby breathing it into his lungs. If your child's skin appears to be dry or chafed, use baby oil or diaper-rash cream, but also apply these sparingly to avoid clogging the baby's pores.

The **Gerry Cradle Bath** from **Gerico** is a good example of a portable tub. It's lightweight and small, and raises the baby to a higher, easier-to-reach level. Its cradle shape is patented, and its foam-padded back allows the baby to lie back comfortably.

Once the child is able to sit up unsupported you may want to consider the **Bath Ring** by **The Baby Sitter.** It's ideal for babies six months of age and up, and convenient for parents. Instead of straining your back while holding the baby still during bathtime, the Safety Bath Ring supports and secures the child. Extra large suction cups hold the circular, strapless

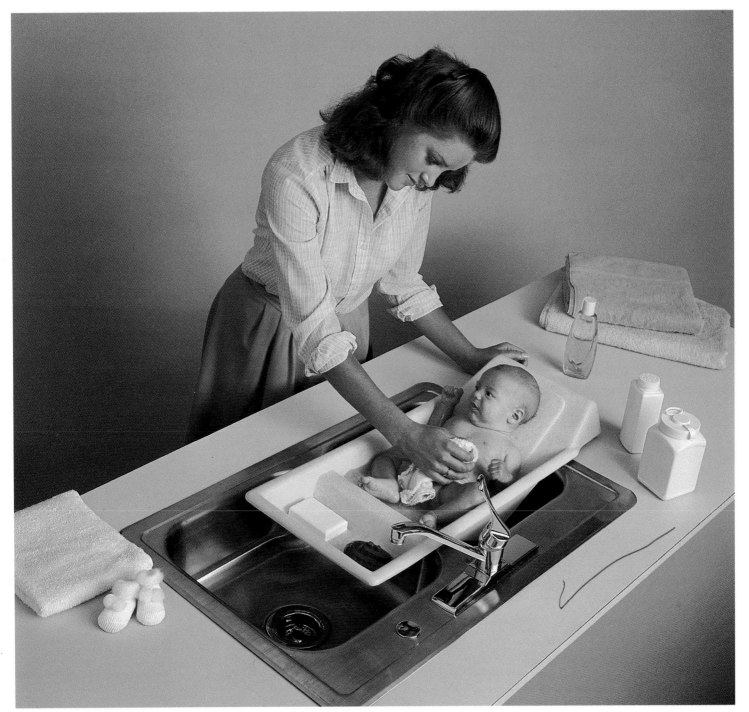

GERRY CRADLE BATH BY GERICO

frame firmly and safely on the tub's surface. The frame and suction are sturdy and secure so a baby won't be able to loosen them. Bathe the child, then sit back and watch him splash and play with his toys.

PARENTS ADVISE

Plastic strainers, sponges, plastic bottles, and cups all make great bath toys.—CG

Baby brush and comb sets have soft, gentle bristles that won't harm your child's head. A newborn's scalp often scales up, leaving little bits of secretion, but a soft brush accompanied by some soap and water usually takes care of this. You shouldn't use an adult brush or comb for grooming a baby even if you're careful.

Baby nail scissors have a rounded point that makes cutting your child's nails a little less dangerous. Infant nails grow quickly and require cutting often so the baby won't accidently scratch his or her face. You should avoid using adult scissors on baby's hands, because they are clumsy, oversized, and extremely hazardous. **Gerber's Nail Scissors** for babies have rounded tips to protect your child's hands and fingers from injury.

PARENTS ADVISE

If you're nervous about trimming your baby's nails, try cutting them while baby's sleeping. It's a lot easier, and safer when there's no squirming.—PG

After bathing, when baby is all clean and dry, there's nothing cozier than snuggling down into an **After Bath Cover-Up. Absorba** offers a comfy, hooded bath bag that's sewn together at the bottom for extra protection against drafts, and it zippers down the front for easy dressing. Or swaddle your child's noggin as well as his bod in the **Hooded Baby's Bath Towel.** Both are made of 100 percent cotton—nothing but the best for your baby's tender skin.

THE BATH RING BY THE BABY SITTER

BATH SET BY ABSORBA

6

GOING MOBILE

BABY TRANSPORTATION

Once your baby is able to hold its head up without difficulty, it's time to roll. Strollers and carriages and stroller/carriage combinations with the latest innovations in their designs make traveling with your child much less of an ordeal. Lightweight, collapsible models, removable beds, and adjustable handles are just a few of the extras that you'll find advantageous. When traveling by car, car seats especially suited for infants are necessary, and in some places required, even for that first trip home from the hospital. Make sure you buy one that's the proper model for your baby's weight and age. Baby carriers are great for traveling, too, because they allow you the freedom to move and use your arms. Carriers have been around for years, but they, too, have been improved and adapted for modern parents.

STROLLERS

There are basically two types of strollers—standard models and convenience models—but when you walk into your local carriage or stroller shop you'll probably be confronted with a hundred different variations upon these two themes. Standard styles are usually larger and heavier, but feature a wide assortment of extras such as three-position seats, foot warmers, canopies, storage baskets, and adjustable footrests. They're great for rough surfaces and usually look more substantial than convenience models do. Aprica's Prima is an excellent example of a standard-style stroller with all the trimmings.

But you're not going to want to push the Prima on long shopping trips or on and off buses and trains. For those times, convenience-style strollers are more suitable. They're lightweight and collapsible, easy to carry and store. Without a doubt, for a convenience model, the Maclaren Buggy is your best bet. It's extremely light and folds up small, but it's rugged, well-made, and very reasonably priced. The Buggy, however, is not designed for newborns, but for babies five months and older. Aprica features a convenience-style stroller designed for newborns, *The Newborn Elite,* but it's heavier than the Maclaren, doesn't fold as compactly, and is slightly more expensive.

THINGS TO LOOK FOR WHEN CHOOSING A STROLLER
- Look for steel frames, reinforced upholstery, and sturdy wheels and axles.
- Large double wheels provide greater balance and stability.
- Make sure the stroller won't tip over easily.
- Make sure your baby won't wiggle out of the safety belt or be able to release the lock.
- Always use the safety straps.
- The stroller should have safety brakes.
- Handles should be high enough or adjustable to prevent unnecessary back strain on the parent.
- Swivel wheels make maneuvering the stroller easier.
- Make sure there are no sharp edges or abrasive surfaces that could harm baby's hands or face.

PARENTS ADVISE

Before you buy a stroller, it's a good idea to test it first with the baby in it, just to make sure baby can't wiggle out of it or tip it over.—BM

The Prima, Aprica's latest stroller, combines the best features of the company's earlier model with new innovations. Ideal for city parents, the stroller is constructed with reinforced upholstery and heavy-duty wheels and axles for rough or uneven pavement. A safety strap keeps the baby securely and comfortably in the seat. The seat features three positions—sleeping, sitting, or semireclining. Adjustable, telescopic handle allows you to push the stroller from behind the canopy or from the front, carriage-style, so you can keep an eye on the baby. Double swivel wheels on all four sides give a smoother ride and simplify handling, while the larger rear wheels make climbing curbs easier. The canopy is adjustable and adorable with plenty of headroom for the growing baby. This model is suitable for newborns to four year olds.

The **Maclaren Deluxe Lie-Back Buggy** is preferred by most parents for its convenience, design, and durability. Made in England, this lightweight baby buggy features a two-position seat with a comfortable, but sturdy, padded back, double wheels on all four sides, front swivel wheels for easy handling, a three-point safety belt, and safety brakes on both sides to prevent accidental rolling or tipping. The handles are extra long, and the entire stroller folds small for easy portability. The Maclaren is lightweight but rugged, ideal for city and suburb. A sunshield and detachable tray are also available, and the Maclaren Muff, which keeps your baby warm in chilly weather. This model is for babies five months and older.

The Double Buggy, also by **Maclaren,** provides parents with the ease and convenience of a single stroller in a buggy built for two. The handles are high to prevent back strain, the swivel wheels are sturdy and rugged for rough or uneven surfaces, and the entire buggy folds down easily and compactly. It's great for twins or if you have two children only a few years apart. A sunshield for the Double Buggy is also available.

The Newborn Elite Stroller by **Aprica,** weighing in at approximately thirteen pounds, folds compactly for easy portability and is suitable for newborn babies to three year old. Features include strong double wheels on all four sides, an adjustable foot rest, a padded safety bar, a safety belt, and a comfortable three-position seat. The handle is adjustable, and a canvas sunshield and muff for baby are also included. It's heavier than the Maclaren buggy and more expensive, but because it has a three-position reclining seat, it is suitable for a newborn.

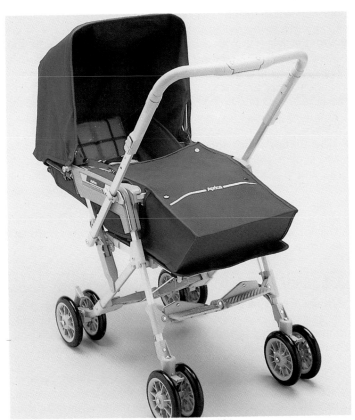

THE PRIMA BY APRICA

DELUXE LIE-BACK BUGGY BY MACLAREN

For something a little less expensive, try **Perego's Umbrella Strollers.** They're heavier than the Maclaren, and they don't fold as compactly, but the two models offered are available with either a three position seat suitable for newborns or a semi-reclining seat for older babies. The seats have vinyl padding and are available in a variety of styles. Double wheels make maneuvering around corners or potholes less trying, but the handles are not adjustable.

CARRIAGES OR PRAMS

If you're planning to take lots of leisurely strolls in the park or short walks down shady lanes, you'll want your newborn to ride in style. In this case, you should consider a full-sized baby carriage. These show prams or nanny carriages provide luxurious service for your infant. Silver Cross of England and Streng from Germany both offer full lines of fashionable, finely crafted coaches for babies. These two companies also make stroller/pram combinations which will give you an air of sophistication, as well as a choice in how you'd like your baby to travel.

THINGS TO LOOK FOR IN THE BEST CARRIAGE FOR YOU

• Look for sturdy construction in both the coach and chassis of the carriage or pram.
• Make sure fabric is durable and weather resistant.
• Suspension points should be securely locked in place while in use, so they will not fold unexpectedly.
• Make sure suspension is first-rate so the carriage won't tip over.
• Make sure there are no sharp, exposed edges.
• Never leave your baby unattended.

The **Maclaren Convertible Pram Buggy** provides three modes of transportation in one convenient, top quality unit. As a pram, the Maclaren features a multiposition mattress that allows your baby the option of sitting up or sleeping. The bed of the carriage, with large handles on the sides, lifts out easily and quickly becomes a convenient carry bed. Remove the bed and attach the comfortably padded seat to the frame of the pram and you have a reclining buggy. The beauty of the convertible pram buggy is that it grows with your child from the first day of birth. The pram and carry bed are ideal for newborns, and the stroller is perfect for three month olds and on. Maclaren's entire line of baby transportation is highly recommended for durability, looks, convenience, and sturdy construction, all at a reasonable price.

STRENG

The Limo is made by **Streng** in Germany and features a removable, lightweight bed for visits to grandparents or close friends. Mounted on a solid-steel chassis, the carriage has a belt suspension that distributes baby's weight evenly, gently rocking the baby without tipping. The entire frame folds down, but won't collapse when you don't want it to, with the added feature of a self-adjusting safety lever. The hood is adjustable with an attractive floral print interior and stain-resistant corduroy exterior. The Limo is available in a wide range of fabrics and colors, or with a charming wicker coach. The Limo is suitable for newborns and older children.

The Butterfly Carriage, also by **Streng** becomes a full-sized stroller with a three-position seat, an adjustable footrest, and a padded safety bar. As a carriage, the bed is removable and lightweight, making a convenient carry basket for the baby. The chassis is steel with belt suspension that bounces gently and won't wake a sleeping baby. The model is available in a variety of fabric styles, and Streng products are carried exclusively at Lewis of London.

SILVER CROSS OF ENGLAND

Silver Cross of England, established in 1877, has a full line of nanny carriages that feature quality craftsmanship using choice, high-grade materials. These carriages are both attractive and fashionable, as well as safe and reliable.

One of their most luxurious prams is **The Silver Stream,** which features a shiny, hard-body carriage with a polished finish. The hood and fitted apron are made from fabric by Wardle Storeys, which is stylish and completely waterproof

THE SILVER STREAM BY SILVER CROSS

so your baby will stay safe and warm on cold or blustery days. The chrome chassis has first-rate suspension points which gently rock the baby as you roll along, and the large, silver spoked wheels have self-adjusting brakes. The Silver Stream is class all the way and great for those beautiful, sunny days of strolling in the park.

A fashionable **Stroller/Pram Combination** features everything but the kitchen sink. The three-position bed or stroller seat is removable and can be used as a bassinet-style carrybed for your baby. A windbreaker snaps in and will protect your newborn in chilly winter weather. The canopy is adjustable and fully lined. The rubber wheels are strong and durable, great for strolling in city parks. The classic gray, corduroy exterior with a stitched navy-blue-and-white border is waterproof and easily cleaned. The Silver Cross Stroller/Pram provides versatile, reliable, and stylish service for both you and your baby.

BABY CARRIERS

Baby carriers are becoming increasingly popular as more and more parents take to the great outdoors. Both you and your baby will love the close contact that these carriers allow. The Snugli is one of the finest soft baby carriers on the market, and it can accommodate just about all your baby's needs. The Gerry carrier is the best lightweight frame, backpack-style carrier. With either one, you can travel to places strollers and prams can't go. They're both extremely well-designed and great fun on outings.

IMPORTANT DETAILS ABOUT BABY CARRIERS

- Be sure to follow all instructions for use.
- Do not bend over from the waist—always bend from the knees while wearing a carrier.
- Make sure the seat is deep enough to support baby's back and will grow with your child.
- Make sure the headrest has enough support so baby's head doesn't fall forward or backward.
- Make sure the leg openings are snug enough so legs won't slip out, but sides should be adjustable as baby gets older.
- Shoulder straps should also be adjustable and, preferably, padded.

Give your baby safety and comfort with a **Soft Baby Carrier** from **Snugli**. While you shop, bike, or hike, carry the baby on your back or up front against your shoulder. The shoulder straps are padded and adjustable, and a soft waistband gives you added comfort and support. The baby can either snooze or take in the sights in a comfy, secure inner pouch that adjusts for growth. An outer pouch zips open for easy access and provides the needed back support for your baby. A soft pad gently and warmly supports your baby's head, and the flannel bib conveniently snaps out for easy cleaning. The Snugli has no unfinished edges or abrasive surfaces. The seams are reinforced, and the all-fabric carrier is machine washable. Available in seersucker, denim, and red, blue, or tan corduroy, the Snugli is suitable for newborns to three year olds.

SOFT BABY CARRIER BY SNUGLI

PARENTS ADVISE

In my opinion the Snugli is the best in soft baby carriers because it covers my baby up more than any other carrier. It keeps him warmer and more secure during winter traveling.—LB

CAR SEATS

Car seats should be used for your baby's first trip home from the hospital and for every trip afterward until the baby outgrows the seat. Some infant seats can be used as car seats, but they usually accommodate children only up to about twenty pounds or twenty-six inches, at which point you'll have to purchase a new seat. It's wise, then, to consider a convertible model which can be used for both infants and toddlers.

While traveling with infants, the seat should be facing the rear of the car in a semireclining position. For toddlers, the convertible seats can be faced forward and strap adjustments made for their larger size. No tether is required on most convertible seats, but you may wish to use one, nevertheless, for the added protection.

IMPORTANT THINGS TO CHECK WHEN SELECTING A CAR SEAT

- Look for a sturdy frame, a strong shell, and a high-winged back that protects from the sides as well.
- Make sure the safety belt in your car is long enough to pass through frame of car seat.
- Keep the safety shield buckled down when not in use to prevent it from popping up and obstructing the rear view.
- Fasten the crotch strap short so the lap straps are over baby's thighs.
- On hot days, before placing baby in position, check to make sure the vinyl or metal on the car seat isn't too hot. If seat is too hot, cover it with a cool cloth, or use a car seat cover that won't heat up.
- The seat belt around the car seat should be fastened and refastened each time the seat is used, just to make sure the belt is secure.
- Make sure the seat is suitable for your baby's height and weight and that it meets all federal safety standards.

The **Century 200** has one of the highest ratings of the convertible models on the market. It provides for baby's comfort and parent's convenience. This car seat combines a harness-and-shield design with the safety shield attached to

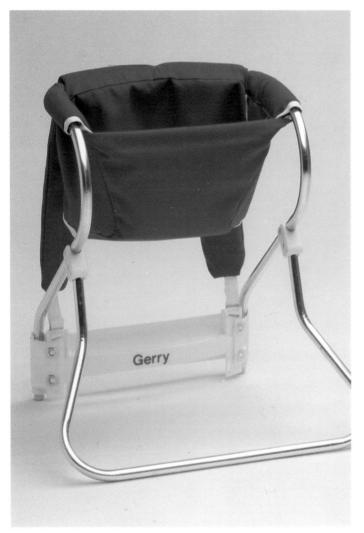

GERRY CARRIER BY GERICO

The **Gerry Carrier** lets you and your baby enjoy the outside world together. A patented wide-frame design is the key to the Gerry carrier's comfortable ride. The baby's weight is distributed evenly, close to your center of gravity. The frame is lightweight and durable with a Springspan, back-bow, shock-absorbent system. The baby can curl up comfortably in the contour seat, which has a safety waist strap for security. Shoulder straps are adjustable and fully padded, with reinforced stitching at all stress points for added stability and comfort. This model is ideal for babies five months and older, and it is available from Gerico.

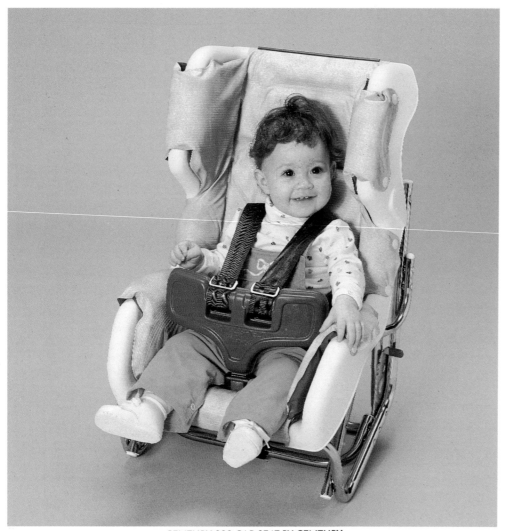

CENTURY 200 CAR SEAT BY CENTURY

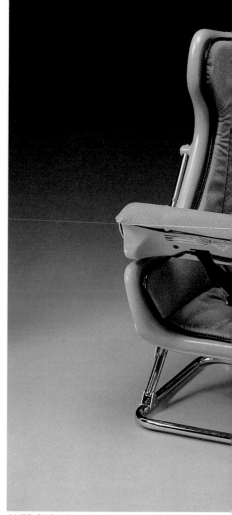

WEE CARE CAR SEAT 618 BY STROLLEE

the shoulder straps at the waist. The shield is an energy-absorbing pad that conforms to your child's shape for comfort and, like a five-point harness, allows the baby freedom for arm and leg movement. Both the harness and the shield can be easily put over the back of the seat while you remove or place the baby in position. The back of the chair is high and winged for added protection of your baby's head.

The one problem with the Century 200 is that the buckle on the seat belts of some cars made in Japan will not pass through the openings on the steel frame, but if the Century 200 does fit your car, it is by far your best bet.

Wee Care Car Seat 618 from **Strollee** is new, improved, and convenient to use. It's five-point harness system holds even the most rambunctious baby securely, but comfortably, in place. The straps are easily unbuckled so the baby doesn't have to be slid into the harness. The soft-vinyl seat is wiped clean easily and features three positions with a convenient one-hand adjustor. A removable, cushioned, cutaway shield provides added protection, as well as supplying an armrest surface for added comfort. Converting from a rear-facing seat for infants to a forward-facing seat for tots up to forty pounds, the seat will grow with your child up until he is four

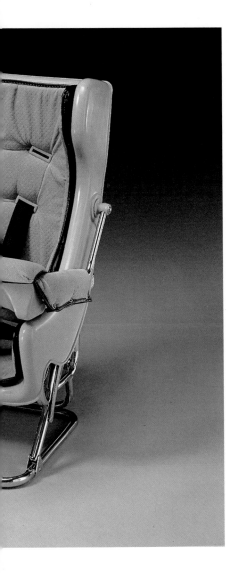

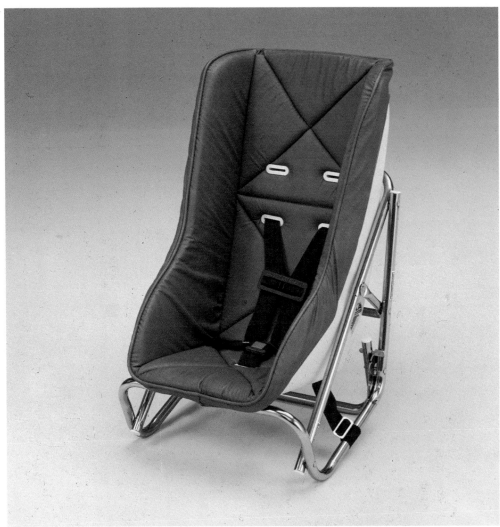

SAFE-T-SEAT BY COSCO/PETERSON

years of age. The Strollee has been dynamically crash tested and meets all federal safety standards. Car seat covers are available in blue velour, gray with blue pinstripes cotton canvas, champagne vinyl, blue terry, and more.

The **Cosco/Peterson Safe-T-Seat** provides another first-rate choice in convertible car seats. Dynamically crash tested, the seat has been approved for use in both automobiles and aircraft. The large molded shell is high-backed and energy absorbent with softly padded upholstery for baby's comfort. No tether is required so there is no need to drill holes

in the backseat shelf of your car; you may wish to do so anyway, however, as it provides just that much more security.

The **Bobob 2** from Holland offers a sleek, stylish look in a child restraint seat. Forward facing only, the two-position seat with one-hand adjustor is suitable for babies nine months and older, from twenty to about forty-three pounds. A molded-plastic shell with a padded interior is mounted on a steel frame. There's nothing smarter than the Bobob 2, distributed by Questor Products, Incorporated, but remember the size and age restrictions before you buy it.

JUST FOR THE FUN OF IT

TOYS AND PLAYTHINGS

LEARNING AND DEVELOPMENT TOYS

Your baby's first year of life is an exciting time, chock-full of discovery about the world. Amazement never ceases for a newborn as each day offers some new and wonderful surprise. Your baby will learn so much so quickly in the first few months of life.

The difference between dark and light is usually the initial distinction a baby makes in those thrilling first days of life. Within weeks, the baby will show an attraction to bright colors. Somewhere around the second month, eyes, mouth, and fingers become the means to explore these newly found fascinations, and the dimensions of shape and size will be added to baby's cognitive list. A baby typically learns to knock, rock, and hit objects during the third month, and somewhere around the fourth month he will be able to catch hold of things with his hands. At this time, a baby is often intrigued by new environments. Try exposing him to new rooms in the house, or possibly, to the great outdoors.

As time goes on, your baby will be constantly and quite naturally learning new things while improving abilities and functions acquired earlier. By the fifth and sixth months, objects start to take on more than one dimension. At this time, many babies begin to acquire an awareness of the cause-and-effect relationship. From seven to nine months, a baby's ability to grasp objects improves tremendously, and crawling on the stomach will give way to exploration on all fours.

At ten months or thereabouts, finger and hand coordination improve greatly. Babies this age are often, though not always, able to stand if you allow them to hold onto the edge of a sofa, chair, or some other sturdy piece of furniture. At eleven months, they'll be packing things in containers, and then removing them again. Increased confidence and self-awareness will also become apparent at this stage. At one year of age, the newest member of your family will be in search of new ideas and ways of looking at the world. The same old things over and over again will no longer satisfy her imagination or her curiosity.

The stages described here are typical for babies during the first year of life. You may see them in your child both later and earlier. In any case, toys for learning and development will help enhance your baby's experience of the shapes, sights, sounds, and textures of life. You'll want to find toys that seriously consider these important stages of development—toys that teach as well as delight. In purchasing toys, it's important to make sure the age level for which the toy was designed is appropriate to your child's age, but pay careful attention to individual interests and activities. He may find captivating games to play with toys that are technically advanced for him—just make sure they are safe. Also, if your baby doesn't seem interested in a certain toy, or has become bored with one, don't be too quick to get rid of it. Sometimes a child will foster or revive curiosity in a plaything that once was regarded with indifference.

◆◆◆◆◆◆◆◆◆◆◆◆◆◆◆◆◆◆◆◆◆◆◆◆◆◆◆◆◆◆

THINGS TO REMEMBER WHEN SELECTING TOYS

- Don't use toys that have sharp edges or corners.
- Avoid giving baby any toys that are brittle or that might shatter.
- Watch out for toys with tiny parts that may come off or get stuck in a baby's throat, nose, or ears.
- Avoid ribbons or strings when buying soft toys; they may get wound around baby's neck.
- Give baby only one or two toys at a time, but change toys frequently.

◆◆◆◆◆◆◆◆◆◆◆◆◆◆◆◆◆◆◆◆◆◆◆◆◆◆◆◆◆◆

Fischerform of Sweden and West Germany offers one of the best lines of "Play and Learn" toys which progresses with your baby's development from the first week of life to the second year. Designed with the latest child development discoveries in mind, the toys are completely safe and unbreakable. They're colored with bright nontoxic paint and will remain cheerful, stimulating companions throughout a child's early years.

As early as the first week, a baby learns to distinguish sounds and the differences between light and dark. Eventually he'll be able to distinguish shapes and different sizes. Approximately during the third month, a baby begins to clutch at things in an attempt to take hold of objects with his hands and individual fingers. Before you know it, by about the tenth month, he's on his way to understanding a number of complex relationships. Fischerform has toys to encourage baby's development at every stage.

The **Cot (Crib) Toy Rod Program** features eleven different toys that help your baby develop each month along the way. Each toy is specially suited to the age and phase of your infant's development. The toy rod and mount easily attach to a crib, high chair, or table.

The **Baby Mirror,** which attaches to the toy mount on your crib, does more than just introduce your baby to vanity. As early as one week old, a baby learns to differentiate between light and dark, and shapes and colors. Nothing will spark his curiosity more than the lively reflections he'll discover in this tiny mirror.

The **Ball Propeller** encourages baby to develop a strong grasp. The brightly colored balls will catch your baby's interest and he'll realize that when he hits the balls with his tiny fists, he makes the propeller move. The toy is great for stimulating the hand/eye coordination that awakens when babies are about two months old.

During the second month, an infant is extremely sensitive to sounds. To encourage your baby to listen, try the **Sun Melody Box.** It's simply designed and vibrantly colored. When you pull the string, your baby eventually reaches up to pull the string herself, a gentle, soft melody plays, and a bright yellow sun rises above the clouds into a beautiful blue sky.

Peekaboo, I see you! The pop up **Jack-in-the-Box** will hold your child's interest for quite a while as, approximately during the sixth month, he shows an increasing desire to explore objects in greater detail. He'll do more than just grasp the tiny

THE COT (CRIB) TOY ROD PROGRAM BY FISCHERFORM

rings and pull. He'll develop more confidence, and will understand now that when he pulls the string a little man will pop up in response.

PARENTS ADVISE

"You can make or improvise your own toys. Try pie tins or key rings, empty boxes to put objects into and dump out again, or pots and pans to bang on for older babies."—JRS

BRIO

Well-designed toys help a baby discover what he can do. They encourage a child's confidence and independence, as well as his awareness and sensitivity. For babies, playing is learning and having fun at the same time.

Brio of Scandinavia designs some of the best and the brightest wooden toys for babies, all made of natural wood and colored with bright, nontoxic paint. Babies tend to prefer wooden toys to plastic ones, because the wood gives more, and is smoother and more pleasing to touch.

Shake, rattle or roll! The **Wooden Stacking Rattle** for infants seven months and older, will appeal to your baby's senses of touch, sight, sound, and texture. She'll love playing with and examining the different shapes and colors as she changes the positions of the pieces. You will see your child show a strong preference for the bright reds, yellows, blues, and greens in the stacking rattle. With growing confidence, she'll begin to study the behavior of the different-sized pieces, which can be passed through one another if moved in a certain way. The stacking rattle is a safe and enjoyable companion for your baby.

Hang it on the pram or stroller and **Jumping Bear** will encourage a baby's understanding of cause-and-effect relationships. When baby pulls the string, the bear's arms and legs fly up in a jolly dancing motion. Jumping Bear's simple design and cheerful brightness will appeal to your child's perceptions of shape and color. It's well-suited for ages three months and older.

The classic **Bell Rattle** is a tiny wooden spool with a silver bell inside. Your child will be delighted to find out that he can create sounds and movements all by himself. Because of its small size, it's a great little toy to have on hand to keep baby entertained during changing time or a visit with friends or relatives. It is best for ages eight months and older.

Also for the pram or crib, the **Band of Bells and Beads** will catch a baby's attention and hold it for some time. He'll be fascinated by the jingles and jolly movement as he either grasps it or knocks it. The gentle motion of a pram or stroller will cause even more eye-catching activity to enhance your baby's ride.

Busy Peek-A-Boo from **Childcraft Education Corporation** is a brightly-colored, happy-faced clown that will delight

WOODEN TOYS BY BRIO

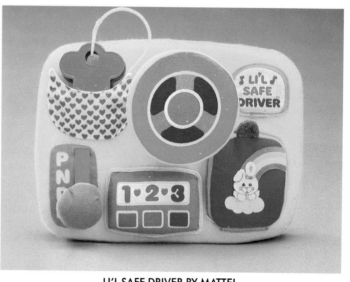

LI'L SAFE DRIVER BY MATTEL

your baby and stimulate his senses. Almost every piece on the clown reacts to your baby's pulls, twists, and tweeks. With a gentle tug on his blue bow tie, Mr. Clown covers his face. A bop on the nose causes even more intriguing action. Busy Peek-A-Boo conveniently attaches to the side of the crib, and is made from nontoxic materials in pieces too large for a baby to swallow. It is suitable for babies from three months to two years.

During bathtime, take the plunge with Sammy Shark, Priscilla Pig, and Drizzle Dragon. They're **Tub Buddies** for your baby, available from **Childcraft Education Corporation**. These fun-loving hand puppets make great washcloths as well, with no removable parts. The entire puppet is machine washable and made of a soft cotton velour.

TWELVE TO EIGHTEEN MONTHS

When he's between twelve and eighteen months old, a child's playing begins to take on new directions. Around this time, he'll enjoy putting things in containers and dumping them out again. He will start to explore and experiment, discovering even greater possibilities. Toys that offer a child even more suggestions for activities and outlets for his imagination are the most fun and educational at this age.

Puck from **Brio** is a brightly colored, adorable dog that has thirteen pieces you can take apart and put back together again. His appealing colors and lovable shape will help your child to accept the greater challenge of reconstructing Puck, as well as reinforce her tactile and visual senses.

The classic design of **Brio's Ring Pyramid** and **Stacking Clown** will satisfy your child's desire to take things apart, then put them back together again. He'll experience a triumphant feeling of success as he recreates the body of the clown or pyramid by slipping the brightly colored rings in place on the spindle. The Stacking Clown has a hand-painted face and has eleven pieces. The Ring Pyramid comes in nine pieces. Other Brio stacking toys include a Rooster and Hen, a Feeding Bottle, an Apple and Pear, and others.

For the best cloth musical mobiles, try **Eden Toys' Dancing Band of Happy-Faced Clowns**. These cheerful, cuddly clowns will entertain your baby as they dance to the tune of "Toyland." The easy wind-up mobile attaches to most cribs.

Also by **Eden Toys** are the downy soft **Chirping Chick** and a cuddly, fuzzy **Rattle Duck**. Both toys are safe and have a pleasing, gentle touch that your baby will fall in love with. The Chirping Chick chirps when you bounce it, and the Rattle Duck has a rattle safely hidden inside with a soft, easy-to-grip handle. Both toys are surface washable.

Many parents think the **Li'l Safe Driver Car Seat Toy** from **Mattel** is worth its weight in gold. Sometimes a baby gets cranky and impatient, strapped into a car seat when his parents are having all the fun up front at the controls. The Li'l Safe Driver gives your child the "keys to the ignition," a wheel that turns, and a gear to shift. A little toy car of his own is parked inside the "glove compartment." The car seat toy has washable parts and makes traveling in the car safer and more fun for everyone. It is suitable for children from nine months to three years old.

Colorful **Soft Blocks** by **Galt** are decorated with a number of different characters and objects. Your child will delight in building towers, castles, or just about any new structure his imagination can cook up. He can sit on the blocks, toss them across the playpen, or stack them, and they'll still maintain their original shape. The soft, washable, and durable blocks measure four square inches and come in a set of six.

As your baby grows, he acquires new creative abilities. At about ten months of age—sometimes sooner, sometimes later—your child may be ready for **Wooden Blocks**. **Childcraft Education Corporation** makes top quality wooden blocks with rounded edges and smooth surfaces from natural grained northern maple. A variety of shapes and sets of blocks are available. For babies just beginning to use wooden blocks, avoid sets with small pieces that could be accidentally swallowed. Make sure you do not introduce wooden blocks too early for they may cause injury. But keep an eye out for your child's signals that he is ready.

SOFT BLOCKS BY GALT

BOOKS FOR BABIES

Babies love to be held and read to. From day one, your baby is responding to all sorts of activity in his surroundings. The sound of your voice and the brightly colored shapes and pictures in books for babies will appeal to your child as early as the first week. Prop a book up in the crib or playpen, or set it up on the changing table or by the tub during bathtime. You'll be surprised to see how quickly the tiniest baby takes to "reading" a nearby book.

The soothing repetition and alliteration found in stories, poems, and nursery rhymes for children encourage the development of important communication skills. Your baby's senses of sight, sound, touch, and even taste are stimulated with the turn of every page.

There are so many books to choose from in children's literature, from the classics to new titles, that it is impossible to list all of them here. The following list, however, provides you with twelve highly recommended classics:

The Real Mother Goose (Rand McNally)

Pat The Bunny by Dorothy Kunhardt and **Pat the Cat** by Edith Kunhardt (Golden Books)

Goodnight Moon by Margaret Wise Brown (Harper & Row)

The Runaway Bunny by Margaret Wise Brown (Harper & Row)

Peter Rabbit by Beatrix Potter (Warne)

The Best Word Book Ever by Richard Scarry (Western)

The Nutshell Library by Maurice Sendak (Harper & Row)

Sam Who Never Forgets by Eve Rice (Penguin)

Good Morning Chick by Mirra Ginsburg (Greenwillow)

Harold and the Purple Crayon by Crockett Johnson (Harper & Row)

I See and **I Hear** by Rachel Isadora (Greenwillow)

I've often ordered books from The Book Stork, a Princeton, New Jersey mail-order service. They have a catalog for $2.00 but also distribute a very helpful, informative newsletter. "The Book Stork Newsletter" comes out quarterly and costs only $10.00 a year. Every eight-page edition includes reviews of new and classic books, a column on an author or illustrator, activity ideas for parents, and reprints of pertinent articles from other publications. It's a real help to parents for sorting through all the books out there.—GF

ACTIVE PLAYTHINGS

Early on, babies will express a desire for motion. It's important, even in the first few months of life, that infants have outlets for their energies. Swings, baby exercisers, walkers, or the even more intriguing equipment at a Playorena or baby gym all help satisfy a baby's need for activity. Active playthings encourage the healthy physical and emotional growth of your baby and will, therefore, play an important role in your child's overall development.

Gerry Bear 3 Baby Swing moves to the gentle sound of a heartbeat as a toy baby bear works its way to the bottom on a weighted pulley. While awake, your child will delight in the little brown bear's progression, but the quiet-ride motor won't disturb a sleeping child. A vinyl seat with pad and safety strap is comfortable, safe, and easily cleaned. The sturdy metal frame is simple in design and provides easy access for removing or placing the baby in the swing.

Strollee Cradle Swing is a large bassinet-style bed suspended on a sturdy frame. Featuring both a sleeping and sitting position, the swing will gently rock your baby for up to forty-five minutes. Available in either champagne vinyl or blue velour, the swing has a charming canopy with fringe. Because of its large size, it's ideal for a porch or veranda, or out on the front lawn on sunny days.

Non-Stop Swing-o-Matic from **Graco** never needs rewinding. The baby swing operates on a C battery and has a quiet ride motor with three speeds that won't disturb a sleeping baby. The molded plastic, padded seat easily wipes clean and provides easy access for the parent. The white, enameled, tubular steel frame is sturdy and durable. Mothers can be confident that their babies are happy and safe, and they won't have to interrupt other tasks to rewind the motor.

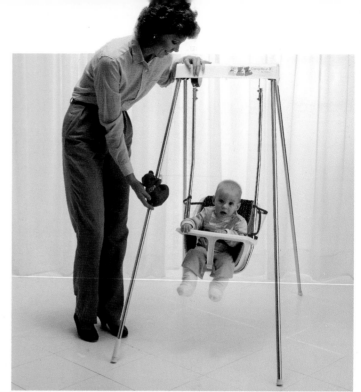

GERRY BEAR 3 BABY SWING BY GERICO

PARENTS ADVISE

I've found that the battery-run Swing-o-Matic is much more convenient than other manually operated swings. Babies are only in swings until they are four or five months old and only for a few hours a day, if that. Batteries are reasonably priced and long lasting. I went through only two batteries before my baby outgrew the swing.—ML

First developed in 1958, the **Jolly Jumper** is the original and unbeatable **Baby Exerciser**. The exerciser is unique in design and craftsmanship: the baby stands in the exerciser's saddle instead of sitting upright. A baby's weight is off his spine and forward on the tummy—as if he were being held against your shoulder. Great for developing strong muscles, coordination and balance, the Jolly Jumper offers an enjoyable and intriguing outlet for your active baby's energy.

The safety of the Jolly Jumper is guaranteed. There is no whiplash response, just a gentle, light reaction to your baby's kicks. Your child is allowed complete freedom of movement and breathing. Swivel snaps prevent the support chain from twisting, and a wooden crossbar keeps suspension strands

CRADLE SWING BY STROLLEE

away from the baby's face. The Jolly Jumper easily attaches to almost any door frame and can be moved from place to place. The saddle, made of washable, durable fabric, is adjustable. The jumper will support up to one hundred pounds and is generally recommended for babies three months to walking age.

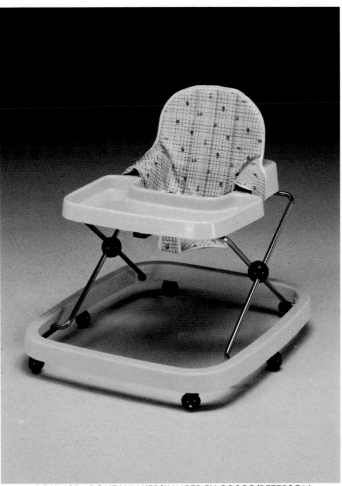

BOUNCE ABOUT WALKER/JUMPER BY COSCO/PETERSON

PARENTS ADVISE

I am confident my baby is safe when he's in the Jolly Jumper: I can keep an eye on him while I do other things around the house, or I can just sit and relax with a good book.—TL

Just for kicks, your baby will delight in the **Bounce About Walker/Jumper** by **Cosco/Peterson**. There are no visible springs, but your baby's kicks will create a gentle bouncing motion he will love. A two-position high-back seat is padded in a cheerful "Happy-Go-Lucky" pattern. There are six wheels, a wide rounded base, and a deep-dish feeding tray.

Walkers are often a baby's first shot at aerobic exercise. Safe walkers, ones with wide frame support, will help to build a baby's confidence while allowing her the enjoyment of setting herself in motion. Jumping, bouncing, and "walking" are favorite pastimes of most babies, but only if there's a sure sense of security and protection surrounding these activities. Good-quality walkers provide that stability. Many models feature a detachable feeding tray that provides a handy dining area as well as a play surface for the baby.

THINGS TO LOOK FOR WHEN CHOOSING A WALKER
- Wheels should be wider than frame.
- Make sure walkers have locking devices to prevent accidental folding.
- Springs or sharp edges should not be exposed.
- When using a walker, throw rugs should be removed.
- Stairs should be fenced off.
- Always help a child into the seat of walker. You shouldn't let him get in by himself.

The **Strollee Fun-A-Round Walker** is for babies who just can't seem to get enough. Four brightly colored, heavy-duty, bouncy vinyl rings, which look a little like Lifesaver candies, protect your little adventurer as he scoots about the house to his heart's delight. The rings are mounted on a bright-blue steel frame with six wide wheels. Your baby is seated in the middle of the rings in a comfortable, contoured chair. The Fun-A-Round will no doubt be your baby's best time as he learns the skill of walking on his own.

The **Century Hi-Back Super Coupe Walker** can be adjusted into twenty different heights. It features a quick-lock device that keeps adjusted positions securely in place. There are six wide wheels for balance and an extrawide, catchall feeding tray, which is great on a picnic. The frame is both tip resistant and shock absorbent.

BABY GYMS

It's never too early to introduce your baby to physical fitness. Baby gyms, where babies as young as three months old can go work out with the help of their moms and dads, are the latest rage in many cities and towns across the country. They're great for developing a baby's physical skills, as well as his social skills. Many parents who have attended baby gyms feel that their children have benefited greatly from the classes. It's a learning experience for both parent and child, and an enjoyable time of togetherness, activity, and involvement.

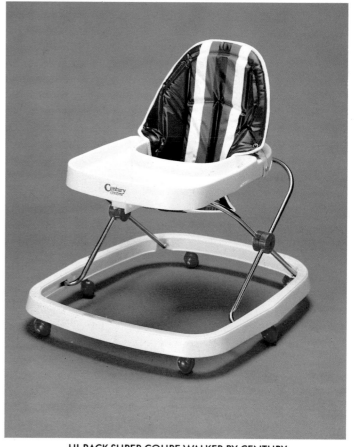

FUN-A-ROUND WALKER BY STROLLEE

HI-BACK SUPER COUPE WALKER BY CENTURY

THE PLAYORENA

The Playorena is the brainchild of former nursery-school teacher Susan Astor and her husband, Michael, a psychologist. Their idea for a planned play environment which stressed "acceptance as the key to growth" began as a toddler program in California, but developed, over a period of ten years, into the present-day Playorena designed for babies as young as three months old.

The program is divided into three separate age levels: "Hello World" (three to twelve months); "Stepping Out" (one to two years); and "Explorer" (two to four years). In addition to the Playorena's trained supervisors, a parent or grandparent accompanies each child to a forty-five-minute class. There are, however, no leaders at the Playorena. Parents and supervisors are there to help and to move along with the child at her own pace; forced learning and competition are not encouraged. The Playorena, instead, gives babies a chance to build self-confidence, a sense of independence, and an ability to accept and enjoy new challenges in a positive, supportive, and fun-filled environment.

Although the approach is intentionally flexible, over fifty pieces of brightly colored specialized play/learning equipment are designed to develop the child's small-muscle coordination, balance, sensory motor skills, and much, much more. When a child enters the Playorena, he's met with a barrage of bright, cheerful colors that immediately spark his curiosity. Once the stretching warm ups and finger exercises are over, there's no way a baby can resist exploring the soft crawl-through tunnels, bouncing on the baby-sized trampoline, or climbing up and down the foam stairs. Near the end of a session, after a period of free play, the children regroup on a colorful, billowy parachute to enjoy songs and finger games suited to their particular age level. Groups are limited in size and there are plenty of activities, so children seldom lack for attention or have to wait their turn.

The Playorena provides an important outlet for your child's needs. While he's having the time of his life, he's also learning important social and communication skills as well as developing physically and emotionally. The program has become increasingly popular in the last few years. The gyms are popping up all over the place. If you'd like to see the kids in action, the Playorena invites you to come, observe, or participate in one of their many Open Houses. For information on how you can join a fourteen-week session, or for a center in your area, call 800-645-PLAY. Or if you're interested in starting a Playorena near where you live, write to: Playorena, Inc., 125 Mineola Avenue, Roslyn Heights, New York 11577 or call 516-621-PLAY.

PLAYORENA

PARENT/INFANT GYM AND SWIM

Many **YMCA's** offer parent-tot classes aimed at developing an infant's muscular skills and coordination, and his social skills and confidence as well. The parent or guardian is required to accompany each child to the class. A YMCA staff member is also on hand.

Programs include **Infant Massage,** which is appropriate for babies one to five months of age and **Parent/Infant Exercises** for babies three to seven months. A **Toddler Gym Class,** which includes use of a variety of safe, brightly colored play equipment, is available for children twelve to seventeen months. **Water Play** classes, for infants three to six months old, teach basic blowing and breathing techniques and help the child overcome any fears he may harbor when it comes to the water. For further information contact the YMCA in your area.

WORKING OUT AT HOME

If you're lucky enough to have a spacious home, you may feel like setting up your own mini-gym. **Childcraft Education Corporation** offers a variety of exercise equipment suitable for children. Try the **Toddler Gym** for ages one year to four years. It's simply designed, but constructed of sturdy hardwood and masonite. Your child can crawl, slide, and climb to his heart's delight. Childcraft also offers easy-to-store **Warm-Up Mats** and **Mini-Trampolines** that won't tip or turn. Make sure you check the age appropriateness of any equipment you purchase and that you and your children read the instructions carefully and use the equipment wisely and with the proper supervision.

IMAGINARY PLAYMATES

Dolls and stuffed animals quickly become a baby's best playmates. They're cuddly and adorable, and will be treasured for a lifetime. When buying dolls or stuffed animals make sure they're made with finished seams. Remember that ribbons or small parts that can fall off can be potentially hazardous to infants.

Babies love to get comfy and snuggle down with a quality bear by Gund. **Gund BabyTime Bears** make up a whole collection of lovable friends especially suited for the newest member of the family. At eight inches tall, Baby Stitch is just the right size for your infant's tiny little arms and hands to hold. The bear is snow-white with embroidered features in pink, blue, or yellow. It's also safe: there are no small parts that will pull off, and the tiny tinkling rattle is safely hidden inside. Like most bears by Gund, Baby Stitch is machine washable.

Terry Bears and **Terry Ducks** from **Marimekko** are Kathe Kruse originals made in Germany. They're adorable, soft, cuddly toys available in an assortment of colors. They make great crib and playpen companions for baby as well as huggable, soft playmates during bathtime. They're washable and available in large and small sizes.

Classics are forever. The classic **Steiff Teddy Bear** is handmade. Synonymous with fine quality, Steiff bears provide lovable, huggable, lifetime companions your baby will treasure even when he's grown up. Every detail is brilliantly executed and finely tuned to evoke your child's love. The bears are surface washable.

A plush, brown-spotted **Giraffe** by **Pupi-Styl** is imported from Italy. The approximately six-foot-tall giraffe has leather hooves and sexy eye lashes. She's ideal for the nursery

BABYTIME BEARS BY GUND

TEDDY BEARS BY STEIFF

(pictured on p. 134), but a little too big for a baby to bring to bed. The giraffe is available exclusively at Lewis of London.

Babies love to look at other babies and they love to watch their reflections in a mirror. Pictures of babies on TV immediately catch their attention. Your child will be equally enchanted by the similarities between himself or herself and the two **Brother and Sister Dolls** by **Childcraft Education Corporation.** Each doll is anatomically correct and wets just like a real baby when fed with the plastic bottle provided. They each have rosy cheeks and loving expressions, and they're adorably dressed in a jacket and diaper set. Made from vinyl, the dolls are 11" tall and suitable for children 3 to 8 years old, but possibly younger. A tiny baby may love the company of a Brother or Sister Doll at naptime.

Stop dragging my heart around! **Raggedy Ann** and **Raggedy Andy Dolls** (see p. 139, also) have that soft, cuddly, ragtag look that children find irresistible. The two-foot-tall dolls are handmade by **Nantucket Designs for Children,** and are dressed in the traditional pinafore and print dress, or sailor suit. Their clothes are made from the finest material printed on imported pima cotton by Liberty of London.

Rebecca Doll by **Pauline** is dressed with old-world charm in a floral lavender pinafore print. She has long sausage curls beneath a straw hat, lavender shoes with delicate bows, and flowers in her hair. Each doll by Pauline has a unique character, name, and dress style. Their faces are hand-painted, so no two dolls are alike. Rebecca is warm and loving and made with fine hand-finished craftsmanship. She measures twenty inches tall. All dolls by Pauline are collectibles and will be treasured by you and your child for years to come.

Happy the Pony from the **Plantation Collection** manufactured by **Klapat Textiles,** has been made with loving care and quality craftsmanship. Constructed from the finest Southern yellow pine, this classic rocking horse features a rich brown mane and tail and an authentic-looking Naugahyde saddle and harness. Rocking horses are not safe for babies to ride without supervision until they reach about two and a half years of age. But if you're sure to hold onto your child while she's on a rocking horse and she seems to be loving it, short rides are great fun. So although your baby won't be riding tall in the saddle for some months, she'll treasure Happy for a lifetime and remember with fondness the fun rides and adventures he provided. Rocking horses also look great in the nursery.

RAGGEDY ANN BY NANTUCKET DESIGNS

HAPPY THE PONY BY KLAPAT TEXTILES

CIRCUS WAGON TOY CHEST BY WOODWARD

TOY CHEST BY CONNER FOREST INDUSTRIES

TOY CHESTS

Although a child may regard his toy chest as a container for all that he considers "fun!," a parent, when purchasing a chest, should make sure it includes certain important safety features. Safety hinges should prevent the lid from slamming down accidentally. Heavier, older chests or trunks should not be used for toys because they often have locks or latches that could keep a baby trapped inside.

Most modern toy chests feature safety hinges without latches or locks. The **Circus Wagon Toy Chest** from **Woodward** in New Hampshire is made from natural wood in a pull-along style with bright red wheels. Red, white, and blue slats are spaced close together to prevent a baby's head or fingers from getting caught between, but wide enough apart to let air in if a child accidentally finds himself inside. The bright red top has no locks, and it features a safety hinge that keeps the lid open. It is also available in designs with soldiers, rag dolls, clowns, and more.

Conner Forest Industries offers an extremely well-built **Toy Chest** with safety hinges and metal-plated joints. The wooden chest has lots of room and can double as an attractive window seat when the lid is closed. The solid siding keeps a child's messy toys hidden and neatly packed away. It's great for small apartments.

Child Craft features sturdy construction, durability, and safety in its spacious **Toy Chests** available in wood, natural or painted white. You can choose any artwork you'd like painted on the front—teddy bears, balloons, flowers—because you design it when you order. There are safety hinges, but no locks, so the lid will stay open when your child has his head in there searching for the perfect toy.

There are alternatives to toy chests. Some parents may prefer open shelves. Just remember not to store heavy objects on open shelves in high places.

Childcraft Education Corporation offers **Open Bins on Wheels** that make great storage areas—you can also easily clean behind them! The wheels are removable, so you can stack the bins or flip them over to use as a table surface. These brightly colored boxes are constructed of sturdy molded plastic and look great in any nursery setting.

PLAY YARDS

Play yards give babies a safe, comfortable area in which to enjoy their toys. Although a baby can be content for a few hours in a play yard, you should never leave her completely unattended. Also, make sure you find a size that's suitable for your home.

Play yards are available with either mesh or wooden sides. Some parents prefer the mesh siding so the baby doesn't hurt his head if he bumps against it. Others prefer wooden sides, because the child can grasp them more easily and learn to pull himself up. Either style is a viable choice because all play yards, no matter what type of siding, have to meet federal safety standards.

Some babies may just refuse to enjoy themselves or to be content in a play yard. Before buying one, borrow a friend's for an afternoon or for a couple of days to make sure your child will be happy. Even if she won't stay in the play yard for long, you should carefully consider how useful having one will be for you. For quick trips to the bathroom you'll know your baby is safe, and when you are cooking dinner, she'll be near you where she can "help" without being in your way.

◆◆◆◆◆◆◆◆◆◆◆◆◆◆◆◆◆◆◆◆◆◆◆◆◆

THINGS TO REMEMBER ABOUT YOUR PLAY YARD

- Mesh netting should have holes that are small enough to keep baby from getting his fingers or buttons caught.
- Never leave baby in a play yard with the side down because your infant may roll into the space between the loose mesh netting and the pad, which could cause suffocation.

PLAY YARD BY COLLIER KEYWORTH

- Never allow sharp toys in the play area, and don't tie toys across the top.
- Remove large toys that may help a child climb out.
- Never leave baby unattended and check on him every few minutes.
- Don't let baby chew on vinyl padding.
- When baby is thirty-four inches tall or weighs thirty pounds, he is too big for a play yard.

◆◆◆◆◆◆◆◆◆◆◆◆◆◆◆◆◆◆◆◆◆◆◆◆◆◆◆

Collier Keyworth makes a standard-sized **Play Yard** with a spacious forty-inch by forty-inch interior. The padded floor and railing are covered in a washable cool cotton navy fabric. An additional blue, floral print quilted pad is available for the floor of the play yard. Independent double drop sides make it convenient for parents to lift baby from either side of the play yard. The entire play area is raised from the floor on a sturdy frame with center leg supports for added stability.

The **Brevi Play Yard** measures twenty-eight inches by thirty-six inches, making it ideal for small apartments. Two wheels at one end of the base of the play yard allow for easy movement from one part of the room to the other. The railing is thickly padded and there are four pull-me-up rings along the inside to help baby stand. The mesh siding is in a small weave so babies won't get their fingers caught. The floor is padded with a terry cloth cover; and the playpen is available in navy blue, white, or beige.

The **Commuter Play Yard** is great for parents on-the-go. This twenty-four-by-thirty-inch play yard is functional and decorative. It's the first play yard that folds so small it fits into its own carrying case, so is always ready for traveling. The play floor and rails are softly padded, and there are no exposed pinch points or sharp edges. The siding is an adorable baby blue mesh. The stylish navy case is durable and has a large out-side pocket for storing a few of your baby's playthings. The commuter play yard is manufac-tured by the **Newborne Company.**

COMMUTER PLAY YARD BY THE NEWBORNE COMPANY

8

A TOUCH OF CLASS

SILVER AND CHINA COLLECTIBLES

How important it is to express your baby's individuality when you're thinking in terms of a lifetime! Silver and china pieces are often the first enduring gifts of a baby's many marvelous treasures. They're gifts of beauty and investments in love exclusively designed for your child. Years from now, you and your baby will be able to share in the elegance of the silver and china you buy today. The following pieces are suggestions of exquisitely crafted, impeccably finished, once-in-a-lifetime gifts for your new baby.

Silver is synonymous with fine quality. The hand-crafted pieces from **Cartier's Silver Collection** are exquisite investments in your baby's future. The leaf design handle of the porringer is brilliantly executed, and the blunt-edged set of knife, fork, and spoon for children is impeccably finished. Sterling silver baby cups are outstanding for their quality, even among priceless antiques. The aesthetic beauty of Cartier's entire collection will make fine silver a very special part of your baby's life.

A classic in our time, **Wedgwood's** three-piece **Child Set** is decorated with some of the text and the characters from Beatrix Potter's Peter Rabbit. The intricacy and colorful delicacy of the mug and baby's feeding bowl and dish will intrigue you and nourish your baby's imagination. Each piece can be bought separately, or as a three-piece set.

Royal Doulton's complete "Bunnykins" **Feeding Set** is ideal for introducing your baby to life's finer tastes. Colorfully decorated with cheerful scenes of romping bunnies, the set will delight your child as well as make an excellent addition to a precious collection of heirlooms. The complete set includes a baby's mug, a feeding bowl, and a plate. A "Bunnykins" **Gift Set** is also available, which includes a baby's dish and a blunt-edged sterling silver fork and spoon.

Johnson Brothers China, made in England for Tiffany, puts a sense of tradition and fine craftsmanship at your baby's fingertips. The deep greens and browns of the elaborate leaf-and-squirrel pattern are reminiscent of Sherwood Forest and the days of yore. Every detail of the three-piece **Feeding Set** is rich and distinctive, extending a special and personal dinner invitation to your beautiful baby.

Kermit the Frog, Big Bird, and all the rest of the colorful personalities from Sesame Street make familiar dining companions for your child as they strut their stuff across the mug,

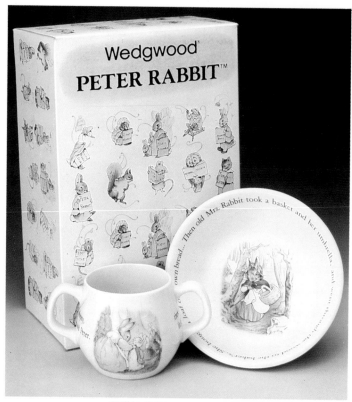

CHINA SET BY WEDGWOOD

"BUNNYKINS" GIFT SET BY ROYAL DOULTON

FEEDING SET BY GORHAM

STERLING SILVER BABY CUPS BY REED AND BARTON

the bowl, and the plate of **Gorham's** three-piece **Feeding Set**. Your child will agree that these guys are at home everywhere, but look especially wonderful on his own china on his own high-chair feeding tray.

Another three-piece **Feeding Set** from **Gorham** is tastefully decorated with Norman Rockwell's *Spring Duet*. The freshness and playful whimsy of an American classic will enhance your baby's feeding time and will remind you of the gentle, carefree days of youth. An excellent addition to your baby's many treasures, the set is practical as well as beautiful.

Your child's own creative good taste will insist upon **Gorham's Three-Part Plate** at dinnertime. It's charmingly decorated with illustrations from Priscilla Hillman's *Merry Mouse Books* and conveniently allows your baby to separate the peas from the carrots. Practicality, charm, and quality is always a winning combination for new moms and dads, as well as for new babies.

Introduce your baby to the alphabet right away. **Cartier's ABC Cup and Porringer** for children will teach as well as delight. Both have the letters of the alphabet around the sides in red, white, and blue enamel. The lines are simple, and classically styled. The pieces are practical, but fun with an exquisite reflective finish inside. Another cup and porringer set with delicate enameled flowers adorning the sides instead of letters is also available.

The exquisite luster of **Reed and Barton's Sterling Silver Baby Cups** will reflect the darling twinkle in your baby's eye. The silver cups are superb additions to a baby's treasures; they are available in six- or two-ounce sizes, with either a gilt lining or pink or blue enamel lining.

Royal Doulton's Hug-a-Mug has been thoughtfully designed with your baby in mind. Scenes of cuddly Peter Rabbit adorn the cup, and the handles on either side make it easy for your little one to hold. This piece is a charming, yet practical, keepsake for your baby's early beginnings.

What could be more practical or everlasting than a silver spoon for your loved one? Discriminating tastes will prefer the elegance in design and the purity of purpose in **Tiffany's Sterling Silver Feeding Spoon**. The handle gently curls under, making it easy for your baby to hold, and the bowl of the spoon is generous for all the love your child can handle. This special spoon is available exclusively at Tiffany and Company.

STERLING SILVER BRUSH AND COMB SET BY FORTUNOFF

PARENTS ADVISE

Though it seems ages away, you or your grownup child can use silver items in creative ways. A long, slender feeding spoon can double as a fancy stirrer for party drinks, for example, or cups and porringers can double as classy containers for jewelry. Then, before you know it, your child will be using these cherished items for your grandchild!—ES

For the first few months of your baby's life indulge both your baby and yourself. **Cartier's Sterling Silver Teething Ring and Rattle** is a classic piece of long-standing tradition. The ring is especially styled for your baby with your child's initials finely engraved inside. A pink or blue ribbon adds the crowning touch to this once-in-a-lifetime gift.

A **Sterling Silver Barbell Rattle,** available exclusively at **Tiffany and Company,** is an extraordinary choice for baby's playtime. Classically simple and brilliantly executed, this precious toy is easy for baby to grip at either end. It is an ideal gift for baby's first Christmas.

Your beautiful baby girl's toilette will take an elegant turn with this two-piece **Sterling Silver Brush and Comb Set.** The gentle bristles are especially suited for tender tots. On both pieces, the borders are tastefully accented and flawlessly

BUNNY BANK BY REED AND BARTON

designed by experienced craftsmen. For handsome young boys, a matching set is available with a military brush and comb. Both are sold at **Fortunoff**, with the option for engraving at no extra charge.

Start saving your pennies now with an adorable silverplated **"Bunny" Bank** from **Reed and Barton**. The surface is tarnish-protected and requires cleaning with a soft damp cloth. It is a charming piece for any baby's nursery and not a bad piece to have around, economically speaking. Before you know it, your youngster will be hopping all the way to the bank. A **"Piggy" Bank** is also available.

Tiffany offers a unique gift idea and an unusual heirloom to add to your baby's collection. A **"The Cow Jumped Over the Moon" Sterling Silver Bookmark** is the essence of fine quality and superb craftsmanship. This precious silver piece

will add elegance and a timeless beauty to any dog-eared copy of *Mother Goose*. It is ideal for your future eager reader.

Evyan offers **Victorian-Style Frames** in both sterling silver and brass. They are elaborately detailed and finely crafted with a sense of history and tradition. In this frame, an air of dignity and richness will surround the portrait of the newest member in your family. The regal pattern designates fine quality, for you want nothing but the very best for your baby's picture.

The classic lines of the **Tiffany Sterling Silver Picture Frame** will surround your baby's precious smile in elegance. The love mirrored in your child's eyes will be enhanced by the understated beauty of this ribbed design frame. Formal portraits or candid photos are transformed into luxurious heirlooms you'll value for a lifetime.

STERLING SILVER PICTURE FRAME BY FORTUNOFF

Fortunoff's Sterling Silver Picture Frame is a birth record and picture frame in one. Suitable for engraving, the frame has spaces for you to record your baby's name, time of arrival, date of birth, and weight, which Fortunoff will do at no extra charge.

An investment in the **Porcelain Cabbage Patch Kid** is an investment in love. This irresistible doll is even more tempting with its luxurious procelain finish. Adorable and cuddly to the last, the china Cabbage Patch Kid will be a friend to your little baby for a lifetime.

PORCELAIN CABBAGE PATCH DOLL BY COLECO INDUSTRIES

Jennifer Loomis
December the twenty-sixth
1982

Mr. and Mrs. William R. Loomis, Jr.

Ann and Scott Kurtz
announce the birth
of their son
Douglas Adam
September 12, 1986
8 lbs., 3 oz.

9

REMEMBER WHEN

ANNOUNCEMENTS AND MEMENTOS

BABY JOURNALS

Your baby's birth and first years are made up of so many special moments you'll never want to forget. Baby Journals allow you to record those happy occasions all in one precious volume, so you can both share in the memories over and over again in the years to come.

Bringing Up Baby from **Palm Press** is a chic combination calendar/recordkeeper for your baby's first year. There is plenty of blank space for recording the important events of each day, and twelve attractive and fresh photos adorn each month. Important milestones in your child's life—first smile, first tooth, first step—can be noted here for posterity. There's also room for pictures of Mom during her pregnancy and—sometimes even more memorable—pictures of Dad during Mom's pregnancy. There's a place to record the family tree, your baby's birth information, and world events at the time of your baby's arrival—who is president, what's the top tune, where are hemline lengths, what are the fads, and much more. "Bringing Up Baby" is a useful and entertaining calendar and journal in one attractive package for proud, nostalgic mommas and poppas.

New York's Metropolitan Museum of Art offers a stylish, yet traditional line of **Stationery Items** with full-color illustrations adapted from *Le Journal de bebe,* a French baby book originally published in Paris in 1914. Charming border illustrations finely recreated by artist-writer Madeleine Franc-Nohain depict warm, meaningful scenes of your baby's arrival and development. Headings mark significant events in your baby's growing years—Baby Is Born, Baby's First Words, Baby Walks Alone—conjuring up memories of moments you'll never want to forget. *Baby's Journal* comes in both Deluxe (Blue suede stamped in gold) and hardcover editions.

The museum also offers *Le Journal de bebe* notecards suitable for birth announcements or thank-you cards, a calendar of baby's first year, and a baby photo album.

Every grandmother treasures the birth of her newest granddaughter or grandson. **Grandmother Remembers** from **Meadowbrook Press** provides her with a beautifully illustrated volume in which to record such happy events. There's plenty of room for family anecdotes and old family photos. Moments only a grandmother may remember will be captured in this volume and passed on to each generation.

BIRTH ANNOUNCEMENTS

Baby announcements are special keepsakes proclaiming the arrival of your new baby. Although many of your friends and relatives will receive the first announcement by telephone or by word of mouth, they'll be delighted to receive something a little more official and lasting. You, too, will be able to save the announcements you choose. Memories begin to fade as time goes by. By saving announcements or those of your friends, you'll be able to recall more easily these important milestones of life.

Announcements are usually printed or engraved. You should visit a stationer or an engraver a few weeks before or immediately after your baby's arrival. Once your baby is born and you've chosen a name, announcements will be ready within three weeks, at the latest.

In almost every case, samples from stationers or engravers are suggestions. A wide selection of lettering styles, designs, colors, and paper grades is at your disposal. Wording may usually be switched, omitted, or changed. Such flexibility makes the announcement of an adoption easy. Simply substitute the word adoption for birth.

Parents should not worry that sending birth announcements will make recipients feel obligated to send a gift. There is no obligation for them to do so. It is considerate, however, for close friends and relatives to return a note of congratulations in response.

announcing
michael lawrence

born september 24, 1987
6 pounds, 8 ounces

karen and peter eastman
321 westfield parkway
cleveland, ohio

Welcoming!

Christopher Michael

May 19, 1986
10 lbs., 2 oz.

Janet and Dave Miller

It's a boy!

ANNOUNCEMENTS BY INVITATIONS BY CHASE

PARENTS ADVISE

I made my own birth announcements. The first time I made copies of the baby's birth certificate, and the second time, I had his foot printed on the front of small cards and wrote a message inside—IQ

On the big day make a big hit with these oversized baby **Announcements** from **Invitations by Chase.** Cheerful red balloons float through the sky to herald your baby's arrival. They're eight-and-a-quarter-inch square, posterlike announcements. Your baby's name, weight, and date of birth appear in red lettering. Put 'em up all over town! They come with their own white envelopes.

Chase also offers smaller-sized **Announcements** in a number of different styles. Mr. Giraffe can welcome your baby into its new world. Or, you can choose something a little more trendy like the pastel crayons dashing the message "It's A Girl" on front. Or, go with a simple postcard style announcement with just the facts on front and a soft, subtle, heart pattern in the background. A number of different designs are available for your selection along with a series of lettering styles.

"Knit one, pearl two, guess who." To announce your baby's arrival, try these adorable **Notecards** by **Calligraphers' Ink.** Pink or blue threads are cast on little wooden knitting needles in either cherry, blue, red, or ultramarine. Baby's name, date of birth, and parents' names are in black calligraphy on white with the knitting needles in the upper left-hand corner. A pink or blue border around the announcement is optional. They are available at Saks Fifth Avenue.

A delicate floral decoration sets off the baby's name, and a lovely ribbon stretches the length of the top border in this classic original **Announcement,** finely crafted by **Calligraphers' Ink.** The ribbon is available in wedgwood, burgundy, or an embroidered variation of ultramarine/red or burgundy/pink. You'll find them at Saks Fifth Avenue.

Jennifer Loomis
December the twenty-sixth
1982

Mr. and Mrs. William R. Loomis, Jr.

Elizabeth Anne London

Mr. & Mrs. John Sims London, Junr.
have the pleasure of
announcing the birth of a daughter
on Saturday, January 29th
1983

Mr. and Mrs. Jeffrey S. Norman
announce the adoption of a son
Lesley Alan Norman
born September 29th, 1982

BABY ANNOUNCEMENTS BY TIFFANY AND CO.

For girls only, a tiny, stitched Raggedy Ann doll holds a white calling card in this colorful **Announcement** by **Calligraphers' Ink**. Doll and card are attached to the larger announcement with the message in black calligraphy on red paper. They, too, are available at Saks Fifth Avenue.

Stationers at Saks Fifth Avenue offer a colorful, fun-loving **Baby Announcement** from **Encore**. Introducing "our new love" in a cheerful, modern style, the announcement includes the baby's name, date of birth, and weight with the names of the parents below that. Red, yellow, and blue trains run the length of the lower border. The total effect is bright, playful, and extremely appropriate for such a happy occasion.

Baby's Hancock monogram is engraved in black on an ecru background in this preppy **Birth Announcement** from **Philip Tripi Engravers**. Beneath the monogram, the announcement is simply worded with baby's name and date of birth. The announcement is blank inside with room for your own personal comments to friends or relatives.

For twins, **Continental Bournique** offers a postcard **Announcement** with two baby engraving plates attached by either pink or blue ribbons. Babies' names, weights, and date of birth appear in royal script on calling cards and parents' names at the base of the larger "Mr. and Mrs." card. Envelopes, either plain or engraved, are also available.

A precious **Baby Announcement** from **Continental Bournique** engravers has an adorable teddy bear in either pink or blue on the front. Nose, eyes, buttons, and foot pads are gold and the bear wears a pink or blue satin bow around its neck. The announcement inside is simply worded and finely engraved in cavalier, shaded Roman lettering. Envelopes are

ANNOUNCEMENTS BY GERD BEYER, INC.

Adam Katz Sinding

Born May 3, 1983 at 5:55 A.M.
9 Pounds, 3 Ounces
20½ Inches Long

Diane Katz Sinding
and James B. Sinding
917 Vernal Avenue
Mill Valley, California 94941
415/383-8590

Ruth Jarmul and Irvin Rosenthal

joyfully announce

the birth of

Rachel Leigh Rosenthal

April 7, 1984

also available, and engravings are done on Crane's 100 percent cotton paper.

Tiffany and Company offers perhaps the most traditional **Baby Announcement.** Each announcement has its own calling card for baby bordered in either pink or blue and attached to the parents' card by a delicate pink, blue, or white satin bow. The lettering is engraved on Crane's 100 percent cotton paper in either ecru or white and often in script or shaded antique Roman-style lettering. Announcements are either in a flat notecard style or folded with room inside to write a personal note.

Old-world craftsmanship is the key to this hand-engraved **Baby Announcement** by noted Manhattan engraver **Gerd Beyer, Incorporated.** On the front cover, baby peeks out from the canopy of an antique baby carriage parked beneath the shade of a tree. The artistic detail is both charming and exquisite. Inside, in avant-garde lettering, the announcement simply includes the baby's name, date of birth, and the baby's weight. The notecard is engraved on Crane's 100 percent cotton paper.

For parents who want a more modern, but simple touch, **Gerd Beyer, Incorporated** offers a tasteful **Announcement** engraved in fine avant-garde or huit lettering which includes only the parents' names, the baby's name, and the date of birth. Colors are reddish-pink or deep blue on an ecru background engraved on Crane's 100 percent cotton paper.

Engraved in lavender with shaded antique Roman lettering, this postcard **Birth Announcement** by **Gerd Beyer, Incorporated,** is simple and informative. A tiny floral emblem sets off the baby's name with the date of birth, weight, and length. Parents' names are also included, as well as their address and phone number.

10

THE LOOKS OF LOVE

STYLISH NURSERIES THAT WORK

The nursery is a very special place in your home. Not only should it be functional and practical, but it should be stylish as well. In the first few years of your baby's life, you're probably going to spend a lot of time here. Playing, sleeping, feeding, and changing all take place in the nursery. It's virtually the center of baby activity.

Form should follow function in the design of your nursery. Furniture that will accommodate your child as she grows is usually a good idea: cribs that convert into youth beds, or dressers that also can be used as changing tables. Waist-level, open shelves in the changing table area will help you keep supplies handy. Don't put heavy objects on high open shelves, however. Make sure rugs are securely fastened to the floor to prevent any accidental falls. The crib should be far enough away from a window so the baby is out of a draft and has no chance to climb or fall out. Many parents install low window guards or safety locks just to be on the safe side. A two-setting nursery lamp is another feature that will make life easier for a parent. The lower setting can be used when you check on your sleeping baby so you don't wake or startle him.

The baby's room should also have its own special charm. Depending on your tastes and needs, this room can be adapted to almost any interior design. Color schemes, lighting, furniture, and floor and window treatments all play a part in the nursery that you create. It's fun and often heartwarming to decorate with pieces that are as irresistible as a wicker Moses basket or as adorable as a teddy bear. Experiment with Victorian touches, contemporary looks, and pastels or bright primary colors. Mix or match, refinish or repaint, but always choose items you're in love with.

The white wicker furniture and the graceful wrought-iron four-poster crib give this room a gentility and lightness that is a joy to grow up in. Each piece is angled to accommodate its function relative to the other pieces in the room—either toward or away from the crib at center stage. It's easy to lift baby from the crib to the changing table, then you only turn on your heel to reach the clothes and supplies in the three-drawer dresser with side-closet. With the crib away from the walls, this room is easy to clean, and the two walls of windows are left unblocked for lots of sunshine. Of course, when your child is older and scrambling around, you will want to push the crib back to open up the center of the room for play. For the first few months, though, convenience for mother is the key, and this setup is superb.

The color scheme takes its cue from the romantic four-poster crib and its lace canopy and skirt. The walls are a soft, light pink with deep burgundy molding. The windows have contemporary-style blinds and are dressed simply in a tightly gathered burgundy ruffle covered with antique lace. The sweetness and charm of this room is finally explicit in the pastel floral pattern of the securely-fastened cushiony rug.

Every piece here has been carefully selected to enhance the room's overall precious quality. The crib linens pick up the pastel blues, pinks, and greens of the rug. The ruffled fabric lamp shade on the tri-level nightstand highlights the gathered window dressing and the ruffled canopy and skirt on the crib. An antique white wicker baby carriage, dressed in dainty blue linens, may serve as a very special bassinet during your baby's first few months, then as a decorative touch. A few toys are scattered enticingly around the room—a pair of adorable dolls on the nightstand, a few playmates on the changing table, and the tiny lamb that lends a Little Bo-Peep touch.

BABYWORKS

he soft, primary colors in the "Gee Gaws" print by **Motif Designs** lends a fresh, pert look to a clean, nursery setting. The dresser, crib, and **Boston Rocker** (see page 53) are in similar shades of white and ivory, and the light passes through a soft white lamp shade, so the lively print takes center stage. The pastel throw rug is pretty and suitable for a nursery, for it is easily removed to accommodate cleaning, moving furniture, or making room for floor activities. The ruffled pillow in the rocker and the pot of geraniums on the windowsill subtly pick up the blue and red in the wallpaper, the fabric of the window shade and the crib comforter. The antique, dark blue toy chest at the foot of the crib is a complete departure from the smart feel of the rest of the room, but its well-used look rescues the space from an unpleasant medicinal quality and ultimately contributes to the minimalist flavor of the nursery. All the different ingredients come together to create an atmosphere that is clean and sleek, but the total look is not overdone.

Furthermore, the careful design of this nursery makes it functional as well as attractive and charming. Notice that the crib is positioned away from the window to keep baby out of drafts, and that the two-way nursery lamp is accessible. The radiator under the window is enclosed in a simple wooden cover, carrying on the design theme, but primarily keeping your curious, crawling sweetheart from harm. Remember to attach lid openers to any old or second-hand toy chests, and make sure they are painted with lead-free paint; you may choose to repaint them, just to be doubly safe. The pillow in the crib, also by Motif Designs, is for purely decorative purposes and should be removed before your infant's bedtime.

Dark tones are carried throughout this **Lewis of London** nursery, but the lighting from the large arched windows in the rear, the white walls, and the pastel and primary color accents give the space a freshness. The beechwood **Nathalie Crib** (see p. 44) takes center stage. It features adjustable mattress heights, ample storage space below, and removable side rails so the crib can later be converted into a youth bed. The dark trim on the arched head- and footboard complements the dark, gracefully curved molding defining the windows. The luxurious wood floors are enriched by the deep tones of the tapestry carpet on top, while the six-foot-tall **Pupi-Styl Giraffe** (see p. 109) draws this richness up above eye level.

The **Cristall** series of **Dresser Drawers** and **Wardrobes** arranged in an arch-like fashion behind the crib also has dark, coordinating trim. The bureaus at the left and right of the picture each have seven drawers and an easily accessible open shelf above. The four-drawer dresser with the small closet beside it also features a removable changing table on top. The charming armoire, with open shelving and drawers, stands behind the crib.

A few plants, if placed carefully at certain safe points in a nursery, add a vitality to the room that's often essential when using dark or natural color schemes. The bright blue rocking hippo, the softly colored arched rainbow wall hanging, and the cheerful **Little Boy Nursery Lamp** are examples of how accessories can be used to lighten a space and save it from becoming overdone.

Space can be the final frontier in a nursery, too. Children need room to play and to grow. The furnishings in this room have been kept to a minimum and have been arranged and selected with your baby in mind. The **Marimekko "Cars and Trucks Grid"** pattern wallpaper reaches three-quarters of the way up the wall; the rest of the wall and ceiling are painted a rich primary blue to create a feeling that you're playing outdoors. The large white Japanese lantern in the center of the room complements the airy, outside feeling of the design scheme. When the baby gets bigger, the bright red play gym at the center will provide a standing invitation for a good time.

In addition to being fun, this nursery is functional. The dresser by the bay window doubles as a changing table surface for the baby. Large open shelves at the foot of the crib allow toys and supplies to be reached easily. The natural wood crib, placed away from the windows, features adjustable mattress settings that will grow as your child does. A contemporary red folding chair is handy and not too imposing.

A nursery built for two! When you have twins or two babies close in age bunking in the same room, you'll want to keep clutter to a minimum and the action on the walls. Here, classic Walt Disney characters, from Pinocchio to Dumbo the Elephant, will become your babies' first friends. They tell stories in bright colors that will stimulate the senses and encourage imagination. The characters dance over and around a colorful rainbow motif that continues across the coordinated window shade.

This nursery easily contains two cribs with storage drawers below, each situated away from the window. (If you use secondhand cribs, make sure the paint is non-toxic and won't chip. If the crib is more than ten years old, you shouldn't use it.) The baby trampoline and yellow teddy playfully offset the cribs. The carpeted floor is left open and uncluttered for plenty of playtime activity.

oo much is just about right in this elaborately styled Victorian-fashion nursery by **Gloria Vanderbilt.** The wallpaper pattern is repeated on both the floor and ceiling, interrupted only by white baseboard molding and window trim. The large pattern makes this small space seem larger than life. The furnishings, however, are not completely lost in the background. The white Victorian wicker, sloped-back chair, and rocker have a character and an undeniable artistic presence all their own. The wicker bassinet is exquisitely dressed in a combination of antique ivory lace and white eyelet with a dainty floral pattern. Swags of lace also adorn the window. The elaborate nightstand and antique Victorian lamp are fetchingly juxtaposed with a picture of an old-fashioned woman presented in a contemporary way. The brass teardrop chandelier hangs away from the baby's bassinet, but provides an added sense of richness to the upper part of the room. The toy chest beneath the window, bleached and painted in the Victorian manner, resembles an oversized treasure chest.

"The Children's Party" Victorian needlepoint rug won't give in to the imposing pattern on the floor it covers. A child's cup and dish and a book of fairy tales are displayed on the end table beside the white rocker. And to add a touch of fitting Gothic romance, the doll seated in the corner has had her eyes on you since you walked in the room. Don't be afraid. She's only minding the baby.

The timeless beauty of this country-style room with Victorian trimmings creates a touching atmosphere so appropriate for a baby's nursery. The Victorian lace curtains and framed oval family photograph above the dresser are reminiscent of generations past, while the beautifully crafted antique cradle lovingly holds your own special member of the new generation.

The dresser, like the cradle, is solidly made and large enough for storing the abundance of clothing and supplies baby requires. A handy linen rack also stands nearby and can be used as both a decorative accessory and a practical fixture for keeping clean diapers or your baby's change of clothes handy. The comfy Victorian-style chair at baby's bedside is just for you. From there you can keep an eye on your sleeping baby or hold him comfortably while you feed him. The blues and reds of the handmade quilt and cradle lining provide graceful accents while the window dressed with lace filters the outside light adoringly into the room. The lines of this nursery style are simple but classic—and there's no denying the shinning beauty of a classic.

A room to grow on! This cheerfully designed nursery by **Lewis of London** features versatile furnishings that will save you precious space. The **Baby Block** (see p. 44) is a self-contained, attractive crib that converts into a junior bed as your child grows older. There are five built-in storage drawers at each end, two drawers at the base of the crib, and two open shelves (not in view) on the sides. The entire unit measures 31 x 81 x 41 inches.

Pictured from left to right, the **Novelle** series of **Furniture** is also available at Lewis of London. Again, each unit is self-contained and provides ample storage space for your nursery needs. The wardrobe at left has a full-length closet, a chest of drawers, and open shelving. The four-drawer dresser beside the wardrobe features a flip-top, comfy changing table that is removable. The taller dresser to the right has seven drawers and a wide, easy-to-reach shelf on top. The handles on all three pieces are easy to grasp.

Your baby will find the color scheme in this nursery especially appealing. The bright red of the Baby Block crib is carried over by the red trim and piping on the dresser drawers and wardrobe. At the foot of the crib, the rattan toy chest (which should be fitted with safety lid openers) comes alive when lined inside with a red fabric. When you open the chest a bright yellow appliqued teddy bear is there to greet you. The colorful rainbow and name plate wall hangings add a personal touch to the room. A classic Raggedy Ann doll (see p. 110), a happy-faced clown, and an overstuffed Leo the Lion all help to make this setting a playful and enjoyable nursery space.

UNITED STATES

ABSORBA
1333 Broadway
New York, NY 10018
(212) 947–6024

APRICA
Merchant's Corp. of America
Box 215
16311 Carmenita Rd.
Cerritos, CA 90701
(213) 404–3773

LAURA ASHLEY
714 Madison Ave.
New York, NY 10021
(212) 371–0606

AU CHAT BOTTE
886 Madison Ave.
New York, NY 10021
(212) 772–7402

BABY'S BEST
Box 10369
Torrance, CA 90505
(213) 378–5216

BABY BJORN OF NORTH AMERICA
Box 1322
Shaker Heights, OH 44120
(216) 662–2922

THE BABY SITTER
Baby Dimensions
Box 25A19
West Los Angeles, CA 90025
(213) 306–5437

BADGER
Div. of Standard Container Corp.
of Edgar, Inc.
Edgar, WI 54426
(715) 352–2311

BELLINI'S
1305 Second Ave.
New York, NY 10021
(212) 517–9233

GERD BEYER, INC.
589 Eighth Ave.
New York, NY
(212) 594–6680

THE BOOK STORK
44 Tee-Ar Pl.
Princeton, NJ 08540
(609) 924–7025
(mail order)

BOTTICELLINO'S
777 Madison Ave.
New York, NY
(212) 628–9001
or
Torie Steele Boutique
414 N. Rodeo Dr.
Beverly Hills, CA 90210
(213) 271–5150

BOWLAND-JACOBS INTERNATIONAL, INC.
Fox Industrial Park
Yorkville, IL 60560
(312) 553–9559

BRASS BED CO. OF AMERICA
2801 E. 11th St.
Los Angeles, CA 90023
(213) 749–1351

BRIO SCANDITOY CORP.
6531 N. Sidney Pl.
Milwaukee, WI 53209
(800) 558–6863, ext. 79

CABBAGE PATCH
Coleco Industries
899 S. Quaker Lane
West Hartford, CT 06107
(203) 522–5175

THE WILLIAM CARTER CO.
963 Highland Ave.
Needham Heights, MA 02194
(617) 444–7500
or
Suite 927
112 W. 34th St.
New York, NY 10001
(212) 868–1600

CARTIER
Fifth Ave. and E. 52nd St.
New York, NY 10022
(212) 753–0111

CENTURY PRODUCTS
1366 Commerce Dr.
Stow, OH 44224
(216) 686–3000

CHASE STATIONERS
Oak St.
Westboro, MA 01581
(617) 366–4441

CHILD CRAFT
Box 444
501 E. Market St.
Salem, IN 47167
(812) 883–3111

CHILDCRAFT TOYS THAT TEACH
Childcraft Education Corporation
20 Kilmer Rd.
Edison, NJ 08818
(201) 572–6100

COLLIER KEYWORTH
One Tuttle Pl.
Gardner, MA 01440
(617) 632–0120

THE COMPANY STORE
Dept. R714
1205 S. Seventh St.
LaCrosse, WI 54601
(800) 356–9367
(mail order)

CONNER FOREST INDUSTRIES
Box 847
Wausau, WI 54401
(715) 842–0511

CONTINENTAL BOURNIQUE
185 Varick St.
New York, NY
(212) 620–0800

COSCO/PETERSON
2525 State St.
Columbus, IN 47201
(812) 372–2154

CREATION STUMMER
112 W. 34th St.
New York, NY 10001
(212) 695–8770

BABY DIOR
Rm. 2400
112 W. 34th St.
New York, NY 10020
(212) 563–9800

CHRISTIAN DIOR, ENFANT
34 W. 33rd St.
New York, NY 10001
(212) 244–6655

DOMINO PATCHWORKS
100 Sixth Ave.
New York, NY 10003
(212) 226–3195

C.B. DUMONT AND CO.
Box 418
Newport, RI 02840
(401) 849–4449

EDEN TOYS
112 W. 34th St.
New York, NY 10120
(212) 564–5980

EVENFLO PRODUCTS CO.
771 N. Freedom
Ravenna, OH 44266
(216) 296–3465

EVYAN PERFUME AND GIFT SHOP
711 Fifth Ave.
New York, NY 10022
(212) 752–0725

THE FIRST YEARS
Kiddie Products, Inc.
One Kiddie Dr.
Avon, MA 02322
(800) 225–0382

FISCHER AMERICA
175 Rte. 46 W.
Fairfield, NJ 07006
(201) 227–9283

FISHER PRICE
200 Fifth Ave.
New York, NY 10010
(212) 675–3939

FORTUNOFF
681 Fifth Ave.
New York, NY 10022
(212) 758–6660

FUSEN USAGI
927 Madison Ave.
New York, NY 10021
(212) 772–6180

JAMES GALT TOYS AND CO., INC.
63 Whitfield St.
Guilford, CT 06437
(203) 453–3366

GALWAY IRISH CRYSTAL
Dept. A
144 Addison St.
Boston, MA 02128
(617) 569–7600

GEAR KIDS
Dundee Mills, Inc.
111 W. 40th St.
New York, NY 10018
(212) 840–7200

GERBER PRODUCTS CO.
112 W. 34th St.
New York, NY 10020
(212) 564–5392

GERRY/GERICO
1250 Broadway
New York, NY 10001
(212) 594–8928

GLENNA JEAN
Box 2187
Petersburg, VA 23804
(804) 861–0687

GORHAM
333 Adelaide St.
Providence, RI 02907
(401) 785–9800

GRACO CHILDREN'S PRODUCTS, INC.
Main St.
Elverson, PA 19520
(215) 286–5952

GUND, INC.
Box H
44 National Rd.
Edison, NJ 08818
(201) 287–0880

INFA
Monterey Labs
Box 15129
Las Vegas, NV 89114
(702) 876–3888

IZOD LTD.
11 Pennsylvania Plaza
New York, NY 10001
(212) 502–3000

KLAPAT TEXTILES
Box 947
Union, SC 29379
(803) 674–5504

LEWIS OF LONDON
215 E. 51st St.
New York, NY 10022
(212) 688–3669

LION'S BABY
Venice Trading Co.
1341 Ocean Ave., #109
Santa Monica, CA 90401
(213) 459–6715
or
112 W. 34th St.
New York, NY 10120
(212) 947–3443

ANDREWS MACLAREN, INC.
Box 2004
Dept. U
New York, NY 10017
(800) 233–1224

THE MARIMEKKO STORE
7 West 56th St.
New York, NY 10019
(212) 581–9616
or
112 W. 34th St.
New York, NY 10001
(212) 244–7560

MATTEL TOY MAKERS
2 Pennsylvania Plaza
New York, NY 10121
(212) 594–9400

MEADOWBROOK PRESS
18318 Minnetonka
Deephaven, MN 55391

METROPOLITAN MUSEUM OF
ART
Fifth Ave. and 82nd St.
New York, NY 10028
(212) 535-7710

MOTIF DESIGNS
20 Jones St.
New Rochelle, NY 10801
(914) 633-1170

MOTHERCARE STORES
529 Fifth Ave.
New York, NY 10017
(212) 557-9400

NANTUCKET DESIGNS
12 Orange St.
Nantucket, MA 02554
(617) 228-2997

NEWBORNE CO.
River Rd.
Worthington, MA 01098
(413) 238-7757

NIKE
3900 S.W. Murray Blvd.
Beaverton, OR 97005
(503) 641-6453

NOEL JOANNA
One Mason St.
Irvine, CA 92718
(800) 854-8760

OSHKOSH B'GOSH, INC.
Box 300
Oshkosh, WI 54902
(414) 231-8800

OZONA
112 W. 34th St.
New York, NY 10120
(212) 947-5611

PALM PRESS
1442A Walnut St.
Berkeley, CA 94709
(415) 486-0502

PARIS INDUSTRIES
Box 250
Paris, ME 04281
(207) 743-5111

DOLLS BY PAULINE
14 Pelham Pkwy.
Pelham Manor, NY 10803
(914) 738-2200

J.C. PENNEY CO., INC.
1301 Sixth Ave.
New York, NY 10019
(212) 957-4321

PEREGO PRODUCTS, INC.
455 Barrel Ave.
Carlstadt, NJ 07072
(201) 935-5055

PETIT BATEAU, U.S.A., INC.
Box 630
104 Friends Ln.
Newtown, PA 18940
(800) 523-8976

PIERRE DEUX
870 Madison Ave.
New York, NY 10021
(212) 570-9343

PLAYORENA
c/o Susan Astor
125 Mineola Ave.
Roslyn Heights, NY 11577
(800) 645-PLAY
(516) 621-PLAY

QUESTOR PRODUCTS, INC.
1801 Commerce Dr.
Piqua, OH 45356
(513) 773-3971

RAINBOW ARTISANS
35 Old Indian Rd.
West Orange, NJ 07052
(201) 731-6721

RED CALLIOPE AND
ASSOCIATES, INC.
13003 S. Figueroa St.
Los Angeles, CA 90061
(213) 516-6100

REED AND BARTON
144 W. Brittania St.
Taunton, MA 02780
(617) 824-6611

RELIANCE PRODUCTS CORP.
Box 1220
108 Mason St.
Woonsocket, RI 02895
(401) 769-8230

ROYAL DOULTON
700 Cottontail Ln.
Somerset, NJ 08873
(201) 356-7880

SAKS FIFTH AVENUE
611 Fifth Ave.
New York, NY 10022
(212) 940-4790

SCHWAB CO., INC.
Box 1414
Cumberland, MD 21502
(301) 729-4488

FAO SCHWARTZ
745 Fifth Ave.
New York, NY 11015
(212) 644-9400

SHEPHERD MFG. CO.
Box 1512
Ogden, Utah 84402
(801) 392-1344

SILHOUETTES
3415 Milton, in Snider Plaza
Dallas, TX 75205
(214) 363-8727
or
1956 W. Gray, in River Oaks
Shopping Ctr.
Houston, TX 77019
(713) 528-2148
(mail order)

SILVER CROSS
c/o Lawrence Wilson and Sons,
Ltd.
Guisely, Leeds LS208LP
ENGLAND

SNUGLI
1212 Kerr Gulch
Evergreen, CO 80439
(303) 526-0131

SPENCER'S, INC.
112 W. 34th St.
New York, NY
(212) 594-7743

STEIFF PLUSH ANIMALS
1107 Broadway
New York, NY 10010
(212) 929-5412

STRENG
Lewis of London
215 E. 51st St.
New York, NY 10022
(212) 688-3669

STROLLEE
19067 S. Reyes Ave.
Compton, CA 90221
(213) 639-9300

TIDYKINS, INC.
112 W. 34th St.
New York, NY 10120
(212) 868-5600

TIFFANY AND CO.
727 Fifth Ave.
New York, NY 10022
(212) 755-8000

TRIPI, INC.
121 Fulton St.
New York, NY 10038
(212) 962-1354

U.S. FURNITURE INDUSTRIES
Box 2127
Highpoint, NC 27261
(919) 885-8026

GLORIA VANDERBILT
1411 Broadway
New York, NY 10018
(212) 921-5656

VISIONS
41 W. 82nd. St., 8D
New York, NY 10024
(212) 874-0486

WEDGWOOD
41 Madison Ave.
New York, NY 10010
(212) 532-5920

WEE CARE
380 Juanita Rd.
Boulder Creek, CA 95006
(408) 338-9328
(mail order)

SYLVIA WHYTE
112 W. 34th St.
New York, NY 10120
(212) 947-2688

WIBBIES
2726 Pittman Dr.
Silver Spring, MD 20910
(301) 565-5176

WOODWARD FURNITURE
Flat St.
Walpole, NH 03608
(603) 756-3622

CANADA
Clothing

AU COIN DES PETITS, INC.
9350 avenue de l'Esplanade
Montréal, PQ H2N 1V6

BOUTIQUE POM'CANELL, INC.
4870 rue Sherbrooke ouest
Montréal, PQ H37 1A4

TONIA'S CHILDREN'S BOUTIQUE
5763 boulevard Decarie
Montréal, PQ H3X 2J4

MADELAINE CHILDREN'S
FASHIONS
106 Yorkville Ave.
Toronto, ON M5R 1B9

CARTER'S CHILDREN'S WEAR
2573 Granville St.
Vancouver, BC V6H 3G7

CHRISTOPHER ROBIN FASHIONS
650 Georgia St. W.
Vancouver, BC V6B 4N7

CZAR NICHOLAS & THE TOAD
2375 41st Ave. W.
Vancouver, BC V6M 2A3

FULVIA'S CHILDREN'S WEAR
5731 Victoria Dr.
Vancouver, BC V5P 3W5

PEPPERMINT TREE CHILDREN'S
WEAR
4243 Dunbar St.
Vancouver, BC V6S 2G1

ROBIN'S SPORTSWEAR OF
CANADA
55 rue Louvain ouest
Montréal, PQ H2N 1A4

Furniture and Accessories

BO PEEP NURSERY PRODUCTS, LTD.
101 Portland St.
Toronto, ON M5V 2N3

RICHARD'S BABIES' PLACE
1242 St. Clair Ave. W.
Toronto, ON M6E 1B7

STORKLAND FURNITURE
1319 Kennedy Rd.
Scarborough, ON M1P 2L6

STORKLAND FURNITURE
3291 Yonge St.
Toronto, ON M4N 2L8

WATCH ME GROW
82 Steeles Ave. W.
Thornhill, ON L4J 1A1

BABY RAMA LTD.
6235 rue Saint-Hubert
Montréal, PQ H2S 2L9

DÉCARIE JUVENILE FURNITURE
5167 boulevard Décarie
Montréal, PQ H3X 2H9

Toys and Playthings

JEUJEU
4972 chemin Queen Mary
Montréal, PQ H3W 1X4

JOLLY JUMPER, INC.
Cambridge, ON N1R 3E2

LITTLE PEOPLE
154 Water St.
Vancouver, BC V6B 1B2

J.A. MERETTE & FILS, INC.
761 rue Villeray
Montreal, PQ H2R 1J2

MR. GAMEWAY'S ARK
675 Yonge St.
Toronto, ON M4L 1J4

MOSTLY DOLLS
353 Eglinton Ave. W.
Toronto, ON M5N 1A3

THE TOY BOX
3010 W. Broadway
Vancouver, BC V6K 2H1

THE TOY CIRCUS
2036 Queen St. E.
Toronto, ON M4L 1J4

THE TOY SHOP
62 Cumberland St.
Toronto, ON M4W 1J4

TOY TOWN
1754 Avenue Rd.
Toronto, ON M5M 3Y9

WINDMILL TOYS
2387 W. 41st Ave.
Vancouver, BC V6M 2A3
and
982 Park Royal S.
West Vancouver, BC V7 T 1A1

INDEX